The Way, The Truth, and The Life Behind Bars
Author: Tim Dorway
Cover artwork by Shane Frederick
Layout and design by Susan Conrad, Amy Hazen and Tony Jones
Editing assistance provided by Kate Dorway
Online assistance: Tina Bruchhauser | iDesign AZ

Copyright © 2020 by Tim Dorwy.
First printing, 2020
ISBN: 978-0-578-53863-1 (Paperback)

To order copies go to:
Amazon.com

The Way,
The Truth,
and The Life
Behind Bars

Preparing for and Surviving
Your Prison Sentence

written by Tim Dorway

cover art by Shane Frederick

INTRODUCTION

You never expected this. I didn't either. But, life happens. And, it is time for us both to admit we are broken, we need help, and we put ourselves in this position. Don't blame anyone else. It is on us. Very likely, this is the end of a long line of traumas you or a loved one suffered and tried to cover up with drugs, alcohol, sex, violence, etc. The saying goes "Hurt people hurt people." Those things, in turn, all come back to get us in the end, and they should. Or, if you are like me, you know that God said "Enough. It's time to break him down and bring him back to me." Whatever you believe, here we are.

Let me give you the best advice I can, advice that will serve you well, as it has served me. DEAL WITH IT. Unless you were truly wronged, which isn't likely, nothing will change your sentence. And should you keep fighting the system, you will just prolong your agony. It is over. You are where you are and need to move forward. Even though it hurts to hear it, you are now referred to as an "offender." Put the past behind you and accept this. In his series on relationships named "Shipwrecked," Pastor Ron Carpenter stated, "Wisdom is the ability to see the opportunities that God provides." Opportunity. That is what is before you.

Now that we have dispatched with the facts, let's move forward with why I put this together. Until I was arrested, I had not spent one second in custody. That was 44 years of being a free man. I had absolutely no clue what to expect, other than what I saw on "Cops." My family tried to plan as best they could, researching and reading in advance.

I talked to ex-cons in my group therapy sessions, read anything I could find and asked my attorney for information. She was awesome and did what she could. But, here is the thing. Neither she, nor any of her colleagues, have ever been to prison. It was all hearsay.

What I have attempted to do is put together for you the nuts and bolts of what I know and see each day, what has helped me most and what I believe is sound advice as you and your loved ones prepare for the time before you. Regardless of what state you are in, much of the information is the same, though some of the verbiage may be different. I wish you the very best as you move through the challenging times ahead. Dedicate yourself to improving your circumstances in the joint. The "world" will be a better place when you walk through those doors for the last time. But for now, you are staring down the door on the way in. Get prepared. Open it. Walk through with confidence. Opportunity.

Peace-
Tim

> "For I know the plans I have for you", declares the Lord, "plans to prosper you and not to harm you, plans to give you hope and a future."
> *Jeremiah 29:11*

THERE ARE NO COINCIDENCES

Something was missing. According to my publisher Tony, it was a "travesty." I thought I had covered everything, day to day prison life, using the throne, finances, communication with family, a support network and even a glossary of prison terms. But, he said I missed the most important part, the part that was my foundation and, possibly, the best part of this whole story. A chapter was missing.

Tony was right.

So, I went back to the drawing board, spent a couple of days in prayer and reflection, and I focused on what REALLY helped me most in getting through each day and continues to help me get through each day. It is no coincidence that every single twelve-

Here is the guy most people thought they knew, Principal Tim. I am still really proud of the work we did for our students and I was blessed to work with so many amazing educators, parents and students. That I let them down is one of my greatest disappointments.

step program (NA, AA, SAA, SOA, GA) speaks of a "higher power" and recognizing that we have lost control of our lives.

I was a hot mess and entirely out of control a good chunk of my adult life and especially in the months and years leading to my arrest. And, even though I thought I had a good start on my faith journey when I was processed at the Department of Corrections, it took me nearly fifteen months of confinement to finally quit fighting "it" nearly every single day, "it" being life in general and the need for control in my life. That is the focus of this chapter, that journey and trust and belief that I was loved, worthwhile and that everything would be just fine.

While understanding how to properly crap in prison was important and likely helped me to avoid many a conflict and more than one physical altercation, the most important chapter in my life and the most important chapter of this book starts here.

This chapter tells the story of my testimony, how I came to know grace and understand how God works in my life and what it finally took for me to let go and hand over the keys to my life to Him. He saved my life and helped me really find hope every day during my criminal proceedings, throughout my prison bit and beyond.

THE FACTS

This won't be easy to read. Hell, it isn't easy to write, but it is important. You need to know the facts of my arrest, my addiction and how I ended up in this place writing a book on preparing for prison when I had never spent a second in handcuffs previously. Maybe you will quit reading when you see the terrible details. I hope not. The story gets better and better as you read.

Before you get to those really hard details, the parts that will make you wince and maybe even close your eyes, I need to clarify something. NONE of what I share is a reason or an excuse for my offense, for creating so many victims, for hurting so many fine people. Period. I am ashamed of the facts and the how and the why. Simply, I didn't know how to cope or deal with the emotions and events of my life, events that every single human being likely experiences. And, I ran to very dark places to avoid being vulnerable with others and to steer clear of coping in a healthy way.

Everything likely looked "perfect" from the outside. That is how I was taught to live from a young age. Everything needed to be just fine. Always. Make sure everything appears perfect. Dress nice. Act nice. Have a big personality. Make people laugh. Host a big party. Work hard. Play hard. Crash at night. Repeat.

In many aspects, my life was dang-near perfect, especially early on. I had a terrific family with an amazing wife and three terrific kids. We had golden retrievers, the family minivan, a fenced-in back yard and a bonfire pit where we gathered together, roasted marshmallows and listened to Miley Cyrus and Los Lonely Boys as a family. It was truly a party in the USA.

Professionally, I spent over twenty years serving students, parents and staff in public education, first as an English/Journalism and speech teacher, then as an assistant principal and, finally, as a high school principal in two different high schools. I coached varsity sports and high school speech. I loved helping people, especially the students and staff.

Even though I had all of those wonderful people and things, I was still missing something very important, someone so, so important. Hold that thought. More on that in a bit.

But, my perfect world really started to crumble as my career and personal life moved along. At least, on the inside it did. Never, of course, where people might see it. Important people in my life passed away, my parents divorced, our family structure fractured. My mother attempted more than once to take her own life. At work, parents attacked, students died of overdoses, budgets were cut, layoffs were required and staff was impacted. I took a new job, moving our family to the metro area again. Our house never sold and we had two mortgages. The foreclosure on our previous home was my fault, I felt. I had an affair and Amy and I divorced. Emotionally, I didn't do well with any of it.

No "good" father, husband or principal would struggle with the emotions of the events happening in my life. I needed to be the rock, let everything roll off my back and just be the good guy. Make people laugh, do more things, buy more things, coach more things, plan another vacation, work an extra job. Laugh. Smile. Lie to myself and others. Everything was JUST FINE. Except, it wasn't. The shame I felt was tearing me apart inside.

Find and read the poem by Stevie Smith entitled "Not Waving, But Drowning." My life. Ironically, I used to teach that poem to high school juniors. I remember it making me emotional every time I taught it. Huh.

So, instead of sharing my emotions with a loved one or close friend or a therapist or with God (I didn't understand that I could tell him everything), I turned to a drug. But, not weed or cocaine or heroin. No, I turned to the internet and, eventually, pornography. I didn't realize it at the time, but the search for something I had never seen before was reformulating my brain just like opiates do. Read the research about pornography addiction and brain scans. Different paths, same result as drug addicts. Pornography clicking and images delays the release of dopamine and prolongs the high.

When I used pornography I felt numb and I forgot about all of the things I wanted to forget about, the angry parents, disappointing my family, the shame of a foreclosure and the anxiety I had about being a porn addict. Hours would go by as I clicked and clicked and clicked.

Well, the "chase" of finding something new and different took a while. But, over time, it worsened. Now is the point where you close your eyes and take a deep breath. Eventually, someone sent me an image of child pornography. I freaked out and destroyed the computer, reported it and swore I would never see anything like that again. Addicts always say that.

Not too long after, it happened again, except this time I remember looking just a little bit longer and then deleting it. Then, not too long after that, I saw more and more and more and actually sought it. No excuse. Terrible. Filthy. Sick.

Yes, I had become "that guy," the one you see on the news all disheveled in the mug shot, the one considered the biggest slime ball of all time, for whom forgiveness should ever be given, the one who watched as pubescent children were stripped bare of their lives and abused in front of a camera, their abuse traded all over the darkest places of the internet forever and ever. And, even when I knew I would eventually get caught, the chase of seeing something new was more important than thinking about the forever consequences for the innocent children in those images or for the absence that would be felt by my children when I was sentenced to 40 months in prison or the trail of destruction I left behind.

The best day of my life was December 13, 2016 when the Bureau of Criminal Apprehension served a search warrant at my door and locked me in the county jail in a Velcro straitjacket. I was set free to finally tell the truth, to be rid of secrets and to remake my life into one that honors my loved ones, the victims of my offense and, most importantly, God.

That is the story of this chapter, the most important chapter, and how I came to trust and know that everything will be just fine, and how to do my time in life, and in prison, with grace, gratitude, joy and love.

ENOUGH

Until my arrest, my life had become all about me and my needs and fueling my ego. Amy, my wife, left me after I had an affair. Who could blame her? She gave me way too many chances to figure it out, but I continued to stumble. I disappointed our children. My actions impacted them immensely. Amy and I did our best to remain friends and co- parent our children, but I remained a hot, steaming mess inside. And, I continued the lies and secrets and sin.

At work, we were doing GREAT things for our students. They were flourishing and being recognized, but I allowed the focus to remain brightly on me and not on them or on our top-notch staff who worked so diligently to make student learning rich and meaningful. Our school was being recognized and I was always there to accept the award instead of stepping aside to let the others doing the real work have the spotlight.

More opportunities rolled in as a result of our successes. Educational leaders toured our school multiple times per week. I was teaching as an adjunct faculty member for two different universities in the evening. We won awards and I was making presentations at the state and national level. A major corporation who designed and sold furniture to schools paid me a good chunk of change to give two, one-hour presentations on how their people could take the educational innovations we were implementing and design and sell better classroom furniture to a changing educational system.

The night before my arrest I was texting with an Associated Press reporter who had been working on a story they had dubbed their "Story of the Year." It featured the mental health programming we were offering in our school and the day-to-day things we did for our students to help relieve their anxiety and stress. The reporter had spent over one year in and out of our school, interviewing students, staff, parents, and mental health professionals. It was a story that would have had impact and created a meaningful dialogue about what schools can do to help kids. Of course, I was front and center in the story. But, it was never printed.

The morning of my arrest I had laid out my suit, a shirt and tie. I polished my shoes. The afternoon of December 13, 2016 I was meeting the Minnesota Commissioner of Education at her office to discuss how we could work together to change the educational system to better serve the needs of students in Minnesota. But, that meeting didn't happen either.

The arrogant ass who often told those educational tours and his staff that he saw "rules as suggestions, unless they were going to put him on the front page of the newspaper," indeed made the front page of the newspaper that day. And, he was the lead story on the broadcast news as well. In just over 72 hours, Tim Dorway had gone from a big deal (just ask him) to unemployed, homeless and living in a seedy Red Roof Inn in Bloomington, MN until he could figure out other living arrangements. And, he was saving plastic forks, napkins and takeout containers because he wasn't sure if/when he might need them.

Tim Dorway was no victim. God had finally said, "Enough."

EARLY INDICATIONS AND GRACE

Oh, there were early indications that something big was about to happen. It is funny once a person is outside of those indications and circumstances how clear that becomes. In the span of just a few years, the following bricks fell in my life. Actually, I need to own this, I knocked them down. Affair, divorce, foreclosure, immense debt, multiple physical moves, a meeting with the Human Resources Director about "rumors," multiple relationships, weight gain and loss, and fracturing of my family. How was "my" way working? Not well, clearly.

On December 11, 2016 (two days before my arrest) I was at Lambeau Field with several close high school friends. The Green Bay Packers were playing the Seattle Seahawks and, in the midst of a GREAT time with my buddies, something happened in the third quarter that literally made me stop and whisper under my breath, "Why are you feeling this way?" I had a terrible sinking feeling of something ominous about going home. No, you Packer haters, it wasn't about the game. They won. It happened twice and I literally had to consciously think about all of the good things I had going in the coming month. Then, I dismissed it and grabbed another beer.

I returned home the next day planned to go on about my life. Before bed that evening, I told a friend that I felt like I really needed to get back to church and that I wanted to become a member at Westwood Community Church and be involved there in some way. In fact, I had spoken with Pastor Joel Johnson twice at Rotary previously and suggested that we get together and talk about it. But, that meeting never came together before my arrest. I went to bed the night of December 12, 2016 not knowing how my life would change the next day.

December 13, 2016. 715 AM. A knock at the door. My son Tony answered it.

It was shortly after my arrest that I truly started my faith journey and walk with Christ. Crazy, insane God "things" happened that I see now were His ways of showing me grace and bringing me along. Before 12/13/16 I had no real concept of grace. I have heard it defined as "unmerited favor." These early indications of grace were just that, completely unmerited favor and love shown to a sinner, an animal whose face was plastered all over the Twin Cities media, his hometown media and the media in every single town where he had worked.

Author Dallas Willard says "Grace is God acting in our life to do what we cannot do on our own." This is the grace that was shown me and continues to be shown to me. I had not been strong enough to get help on my own. So, the Lord intervened and, my word, I am so grateful.

Less than 36 hours after my arrest I first experienced God's grace in a big, big way. A man whom I had only known as Mark (from my Rotary club) somehow managed to get a letter to me in my holding cell. Those of you who have been in a county jail or prison know that mail DOES NOT just get dropped off at the jailhouse door and delivered. It goes through the US Mail or it is destroyed. Well, Mark managed to convince an officer to deliver it to me by hand. I wept as I read the letter from Mark, who essentially told me he loved me and that he would stand by me publicly, guilty or innocent, and lavish his love and God's love on me. I remember saying, through my tears, "There are really good people in this world." Mark visited me that day through the visiting room glass. He prayed over me and shared his testimony with me. This was what GRACE looked like.

On December 15, 2016, my bail was set at $100,000, a ridiculous amount according to everyone in the world except the prosecutor, who said I was a public safety risk. So, I needed to find money to pay the bondsman. Specifically, I needed to pay 10% of that amount so I could be released. I arranged a payment plan and scraped together a satisfactory down payment, signed the paperwork and expected to be released to be with my kids and to work with my attorney. Little did I know that any bond over $25,000 required a co-signer in the state of Minnesota. I had no one. I called my attorney that Friday morning, the 16th, and told him that I was prepared to stay in county jail until my case was resolved. I wasn't going to ask anyone to take a $100,000 chance on me. This wasn't anyone else's fault but mine.

The next morning (12/17/16), my fifth day in the Carver County Jail, an officer came to my cell door and told me the bail bondsman was there to see me. I assumed he was coming to tear up my debit card receipt and tell me to be in contact with him if anything changed. As I approached the visiting area, a second officer stepped in and said, "The bondsman left. He is all set to go." Confused, I asked for clarification. The officer told me that an anonymous person had stepped forward and co-signed on my bail bond. The person wished to remain anonymous but wanted me to know that she/he believed it was "God's will" that I be out to be with my children and to begin treatment. I still have no idea who this person was to this day. Someone, a stranger, had indeed taken out a $100,000 chance on me. Again, GRACE.

After my release, God continued to work in my life in the most apparent and strongest of ways. My new friend Mark stood by me, as he promised he would, and helped me to find temporary and stable housing. He helped coordinate a meeting with Pastor Joel and, in the presence of both, I finally surrendered and admitted my sins and asked for forgiveness.

Pastor Joel assured me I was forgiven by God, who loved me. His only begotten son, Jesus Christ, gave his life so that I might be forgiven. And, once he was physically gone, he sent the Holy Spirit here to live with me and love me, support me, help me and care for me. No matter what else was going on around me, everything would be just fine. For the first time in my life, I could truly TRUST and have FAITH. Joel encouraged me to return to my hotel room that night and get on my knees and confess every single thing on my heart. When I was done doing so, the foot stool was soaked from my tears and I had an indentation from the fabric on my forehead. It was so good.

As Christmas Eve 2016 approached, Mark and his wife Kay shared that they would be leaving to visit family out of state and that they would love for me to host my family at their home to celebrate our Christmas together. They had only really known me for less than a week and they were offering their home to a stranger? Space under their Christmas tree for my gifts to my children? Then, when Mark met with me the date of my arraignment, he brought scripture and asked me to read it aloud to him and explain why I thought he selected those passages. They all had to do with forgiveness, strength, love and GRACE.

On December 26, 2016 a man named David, and a friend of Mark, picked me up and drove me to his home, where I had brunch with him and his wife Mary. They asked about my emotions, my family, my story, my faith. They shared their story with me. They told me I was loved and forgiven and that they would pray about hosting me, a stranger, in their home while I started outpatient treatment and worked through the processes of my case. Shortly after the New Year, I moved into a bedroom in their home and stayed for several months. My children were welcome there and my family was welcomed there. We shared scripture, laughter and love with their family. It was so peaceful and kind. GRACE.

Then there was John, a parent of two Chanhassen High School students who invited me for coffee in his home office, where he proudly displayed a sign on the door that read "Why Worry? God's in Control." He talked about his struggles with chemical use earlier in his life, his diagnosis with terminal cancer and how his faith had helped him in his journey. We prayed together, laughed together and sat in his greenhouse and just breathed in that heavy air. This man hardly knew me. I had met him once. The only thing he really knew about me was what he learned on the news. And, he showed me GRACE.

One last example, an example that I can hardly talk about to this day. Weeks after my arrest, I found out what my son Tony had done the day of my arrest. Tony and Joe (my youngest son) were with me the morning the search warrant was executed. After my interview with the BCA agent, Tony and Joe met with me in the basement. I told them the truth and I told them I would no longer serve as principal at the high school they attended. They both gave me a hug, we exchanged "I love yous" and they left to head to their mother's home.

Well, Tony was adamant that he go to school that morning, the same school where I served as principal and the same school where he and his brother attended and from where his sister Kate had graduated. Shortly after his arrival, there were frantic announcements for staff to attend an emergency staff meeting in the forum. The word was out with kids and all the big wigs were there to talk with staff, the superintendent, PR guy, assistant superintendent and human resources guy. Tony broke into the meeting of the staff, many of whom I had hired and worked with for seven years, all 225 of them. He asked for a moment and stood before them, told them he loved me, that I had so enjoyed working with them and was proud of the work we had done together and that I was so sorry for what they were experiencing as a result of my actions.

It would have been easy for my ex-wife and children to run away from me, to ostracize me and to act like I was an animal. But, they did not. They showed me love and GRACE.

In the span of just one month I learned more about grace than I had in 44 years. Had this not all happened, had God not finally said "Enough," had I not met such amazing people and felt such love in the midst of my brokenness, I am horrified to think where I might be today. I am humbled and so grateful.

FAITH WORK

The more I started to understand about God's grace and love, the more I sought to find out more. The work I did before my sentencing certainly paid off and it opened up a whole world to me, a healthy and loving place to curl up in a ball and just be who I really was. Don't take that to mean that I was doing it well all of the time. No way. It was a daily battle and it continues to be a daily battle.

Mark introduced me to Bible Study Fellowship, a weekly group of men that met to study the Word and lean on one another. My first night there, a man named Scott approached me and introduced himself. He told me that he was sorry for what I was going through it was still all over the news) and that his son had graduated from Chanhassen High School. Before the end of our first meeting, Scott and I agreed to keep in touch. He helped me find amazing worship music, even providing his whole collection of CDs and a boom box (I was forbidden from using any internet-capable device), encouraged me in the Word and shared his own testimony. Scott was with me from that day forward, in friendship, prayer and support for my family and continues to be a major figure in my life.

David invited me to attend Pure Desire, a men's support group for those who have struggled, are struggling or continue to struggle with issues of sexual addiction, temptation and sin. Each week, we gathered in prayer and support and studied curriculum, forming a bond of men who could open up about anything in confidence and love. Many of our curricular readings were rooted in a combination of research and scripture. This group opened up a new world of honesty to me. I was not alone in my struggles. Other men were just as broken as me. Bringing light and vulnerability to our sins each week made it easier to be honest with ourselves and others. How wonderful that freedom felt!

Soon after, word came that there was a small, intimate group of men who were meeting at Westwood Community Church early in the morning on Tuesdays. I jumped at the chance and was told instantly that I was always welcome there. These were men, just like me, who had struggled with pornography or an affair or objectification of women and, get this, we could be honest with one another in all of our struggles. Those men accepted me and I accepted them and a forever bond was formed, a bond that was based in forgiveness, grace and God's love.

For Christmas, my son Joe gifted me a leather-bound journal book, which became my place to jot down notes about scripture, my Bible Study Fellowship, Pure Desire and Westwood accountability group meetings. When I stumbled across something that really gave me hope or faith or showed grace, I wrote it down and, when I was struggling with an upcoming hearing, something in my outpatient treatment or searching for work and having little luck, I turned to those pages. Essentially, they became my coat of armor and shield.

On June 25, 2017 Pastor Joel baptized me in Lake Minnetonka as my support team watched on. It was a last formal, and important, step in preparation for my time in prison. My faith "snowball" continued to get bigger and bigger, gaining more and more substance as it rolled along.

DAILY PRACTICE

Prison is no treat. Don't believe the crap they show you on "60 Days In" and "Locked Up." It is no picnic. You can never take your safety, physical or emotional, for granted and you must be aware at ALL TIMES of your surroundings and those around you. It is exhausting, all of it. The rules, navigating the drama, the fights, the hustling and the constant watching and scrutiny.

And so, having trust and faith and hope is critical. I protected myself by investing daily in practice and I would recommend you do the same. That practice included simple things like listening to worship music each morning over a cup of coffee and a magazine. I also had a "whatever" Bible reading plan recommended to me by Pastor Joel. It went like this. Pick up the Bible, open it and read what is on that random page. Another important part of my regular practice was remaining connected with Westwood. I asked if I could be placed on their mailing list and receive the weekly bulletins, as well as Pastor Joel's weekly message speaking notes. So, I never missed a Sunday service. I just had to read the service. And, it became a really happy practice for me. Plus, I got mail at least once a week! Bonus.

I surrounded myself with positive people who had no intention of going back to prison and EVERY intention of "leaning in" to the treatment program. Many of these same men were strong in their own faith and were approachable, kind and warm. I was drawn to them instantly, even as men who participated in pipe and drum ceremonies or went to the mosque or attended the Jehovah's Witness service on Saturday. Most important to me was the opportunity to be around people who believed in a much higher power, who knew love and forgiveness and who wanted to generally be well.

Last and MOST important in my daily practice was practicing gratitude. By practicing gratitude I don't mean just saying "thank you" when the guy in the chow hall flung some mandarin oranges on my tray and spilled the juice in my taco "meat." I didn't really mean that "thank you." Haha. Okay, I was thankful for the food, just not the combination of mandarin taco meat. Not recommended.

Here is what I mean by gratitude. And, this is an actual message I asked my daughter Kate to place on my "Friends of Tim Dorway" Facebook group on December 19, 2018. Let me first say that I was really, really pissed when I went to my mailbox that day and found a portion of my Grammy's Christmas card had been confiscated. But, on my way back to my cell I found myself saying, "Well, I guess I didn't see that coming, so how can I make the best of this? I certainly can't change it." Here is what I shared.

Family,

The following story still has me smiling and I have been telling it to everyone here. I hope it makes you smile too.

Today I found a Christmas card from my Grammy in my mailbox. Upon opening it, I also found a pink notice from the mail-room entitled "Notice of Non-Delivery of Mail." Tina (the officer in the mail-room) had checked that the mail removed "pertained to contraband and items prohibiting inspection/unable to search." Instant heartache.

Perplexed, I looked for more information. What had Grammy sent? A dollar bill? My favorite glass candy? Her handmade egg noodles? All a no. In the upper right-hand corner was a note from Tina that read "piece of evergreen tree branch taped inside card." Instant laughter and tears of laughter. Grammy clipped off part of her tree for me to smell. How I love that Grammy of mine!

So, realizing that many of the responses Tina gets back from offenders about confiscated items are likely not very kind, I sent a kite back with that pink slip stapled to it.

Here is what I wrote.

"Tina-I am dying laughing, to the point of tears, about the fact my 89 year-old grandmother ('Grammy') taped a branch from her Christmas tree inside my card. This MADE MY DAY. You can dispose of it or, even better, tape it in your work area and enjoy a little piece of the 'north woods.' Grammy lives in a whole-log cabin in AuTrain, MI-two miles off of Lake Superior-on a small lake. Until two years ago, she still heated with logs primarily. Hopefully, she sends us one of her pies next time-stuffed inside her card. Merry Christmas!"

It makes me happy that Tina's life has also been touched by Grammy in the most innocent of ways. Even though I don't have that tree clipping, the card still smells good. FYI, Grammy says she is having a T-bone steak for Christmas. That's my Grammy.

Love you all,
Tim

You see, simple gratitude is pretty easy. But the harder gratitude, I believe, often means taking an obstacle and making it an opportunity and being thankful for that opportunity. Seeing those boulders in the middle of the road of my day and laughing at them and then moving forward was what made my time in prison so much easier. Every day became a twisted, fun adventure. I never knew what might happen next.

GIVING IT AWAY

Honestly, it wasn't easy. Even when I had all of those things
going for me, and while I was still making considerable progress
in my relationship with Christ, I still fought "it" every single day
for the first fifteen months or so of my prison sentence, and I was
MISERABLE. I still thought I needed to be in control. I called my
girlfriend many, many times per day. I tried coordinating my
kids' lives, my girlfriend's life, my life. I was writing a book, going
to school and studying to be a paralegal, working a job in the
prison library and law library.

Little had changed with regard to my power and control issues.
At every point he could, my cellie Ty looked at me and told me
I needed to let go, give my anxieties to God and get my nose in
scripture and prayer more. But, I told him, I had it under control.
He just shook his head and said, "Keep doing it your way, then."

I struggled sleeping, had panic attacks about things I could not
control, worried more and held on tighter. Except, in the end,
I was pushing everything, and a woman I desperately loved,
away. That is, until a weekend in October 2018 when I attended
the REC Retreat (Residents Encountering Christ) and learned
about practicing "metanoia," a Greek word that means "radical
change." It was too late for my relationship with Kellie, but it
wasn't too late to save my life and finally do what Pastor Joel
encouraged me to do....to take my hands off my own steering
wheel of life and let God drive that car for me.

We spent the weekend in a big building on our facility campus (no, this was no retreat at a fancy cabin) in fellowship with men and women from faith communities in our area. There was upgraded chow hall food, worship music, grace, forgiveness, testimonies and love. But, most importantly we participated in an activity that radically changed my life and really got me to let go, to give a lot of my struggles away and finally just enjoy each day as it comes rather than be in control of what happens every minute of every day. My life has not been the same since.

Without giving away all of the wonderful details (we were essentially sworn to secrecy) in hopes that you will experience something similar in your life, I will simply share this. We were encouraged to make a list of all of the obstacles to our happiness and lives that we needed to let go of and change radically. These were the things that led to my offending behavior, to the destruction of my family by my own selfishness, to my separation from Christ and to the harm I have caused myself and so many others.

While "Who You Say I Am" by Hillsong Worship played in the background, I wept and finally let go of it all on one sheet of scratch paper and then transcribed my list onto a block of wood we were provided. Here is what I gave up that day.

Fear. Addiction. Loneliness. Guilt. Shame. Selfishness. Worthlessness. Hopelessness. Rejection. Pride. Envy. Secrets. Control. Greed. Lust.

Quite the list, right? But, we were not done. Every man that day, one by one, took his own block of wood and carefully placed it inside a tattered burlap sack at the foot of the cross. Man, did it look heavy. It was really heavy. And then that sack was burned and all that was left of all of that hurt and burden was ash.

After that retreat, and as I started treatment, I began to see how a lot of those traits fueled my self-centeredness, impatience, lies and alibi-making, entitlement and false pride. In the end, I was learning humility.

Here is the great thing about our God. His son Jesus Christ lived and died for us. He carried that burden, mine, yours, all of ours. And, when we give those things to him, we are all freed of that weight and can finally live in happiness and love.

My life, since that Saturday in October 2018, has not been the same.

"COINCIDENCES"

After I let go of all of that, man did life get easier and happier. And, things made so much more sense to me because I realized I was not in control and God had me exactly where he wanted me for my good and for the good of others. I began to look backward and realize that every single thing happens for a reason, HIS reason.

I used to be that guy who used the phrase "what a coincidence." No longer. There is no such thing as a coincidence and the sooner we all realize that, that we are not in control and that every single step of our lives is calculated to honor Him, the better our lives become.

So, here are some of those "coincidences" I now realize were in place for a reason.

It is no coincidence that Angella Erickson was the prosecutor in my case. She told my attorney from the start that she planned "to make an example of me." I was so pissed at her and such a victim then. You should have heard me talk about her! My daughter even came up with a nasty nickname for her. Ninety-five percent of men charged with my offense in Minnesota are sentenced to probation the first time. But, God didn't want me to have probation. I needed prison and radical change in my life. So, thank you Angella Erickson, for making an example of me. It was for the best.

It is no coincidence someone referred me to Christian Recovery Counseling in Golden Valley, MN to do my outpatient sex offender treatment during my criminal proceedings. It is one of very few Christian-based outpatient sex offender programs in the nation and it happened to be fifteen minutes from my home. On the wall in the waiting room, Jeremiah 29:11 was stenciled, and it is now permanently inked on my right forearm with the word HOPE.

It is no coincidence that I was shipped to MCF-Moose Lake for six weeks after my orientation at MCF-St. Cloud. It made no sense. They didn't have my treatment programming or the two classes that were recommended I should take. I wrote the warden, because I wanted to be in control. Why am I here?

Here is the answer I understand now. So I could hear the testimonies of other men and see the most authentic church services on the face of the Earth....prison church services led by FELONS who had given control of their lives to God. And, I ended up sitting next to Matt Moeller, who was serving a lengthy sentence and connected closely to Westwood Community Church. In fact, Pastor Joel had him call me before my sentencing to talk with my about prison. Insane. A real "God" thing.

It is no coincidence that I was not accepted into Prison Fellowship Academy, a program I researched before my sentencing and told everyone I would be enrolled in. I applied four times and sent an additional two letters to the head of the program begging to be accepted. But, had I been accepted, I would not have been placed in a cell with Ty, my brother from another mother, a man who helped save me so many times, witnessed to me, shared his story and his love and faith. He is a part of my family now. Had I been accepted into Prison Fellowship Academy, we would not have even been in the same treatment unit together, let alone the same cell.

It is no coincidence that I opened precisely to Isaiah 57 on two different days in two ENTIRELY different Bibles during a time that I was struggling most. God wanted me to read it very, very carefully. Clearly. Its message is about sin, confession and redemption.

It is no coincidence that, on the day I wrote Pastor Joel about the need for a sexual addiction, sin and compulsion group at Westwood Community Church, my friend Scott had a random man sit down next to him at Westwood, after the early service, and confess how much he struggles with sex addiction and pornography.

And, lastly, it is no coincidence that I was in a very specific sex offender treatment program at MCF-Lino Lakes with very specific men. I needed to hear their stories. The old Tim was so very good at judging others. I learned from the men in my treatment program and I came to understand their lives and to love them and their stories. I learned about empathy and compassion and forgiveness. I learned to meet men right where they are at and, as Pastor Joel encourages us so often, to "get the love thing right."

The following is the mini life story of a man I was so good at judging initially. After hearing it in front of our treatment community one Tuesday afternoon, I reflected on how much it changed me.

With his permission, this is David's story.

David made me a bit crazy. He always seemed to be the model treatment guy, a treatment "warrior" as they say. He followed all the rules and acted so much better than everyone. He didn't really show emotion. He was hyper-focused on his weight and his appearance, walking circles and circles around our living unit, shirt tucked in and buttoned all the way to the top. He seldom interacted with others. Because I felt judged by David, I judged him harshly in return. How could he act so perfect? He was just like the rest of us.

Except, he wasn't.

David was orphaned shortly after birth with two pretty severe foot and leg deformities. He was nearly two and a half years old, still without corrective surgery, when a missionary couple visited the orphanage and fell in love with him and his spirit. They were told he would likely be too expensive to adopt for a couple on missionary salaries. The corrective surgeries would be very expensive. In fact, his file had been stamped "unsuitable for placement" and the couple was discouraged from adopting him by the officials at the orphanage. The couple insisted, yes, he would be their adopted son.

David was raised in Japan, where his adoptive parents served others in their missionary work. He was so happy to be their son. He had a wonderful childhood, loved school, was outgoing and happy. Grateful. When he was fourteen years old, he saw a job posting at his boarding school seeking a high school boy to privately tutor the English language to a Japanese doctor's children. He applied, was interviewed initially and then called back for a "follow up."

David reported to the home and knocked on the door. The home was massive and opulent. The man who responded to the door invited him in and confided in him that he wanted to hire him. He was there to "meet the children." The doctor took him to another room where "the children" were to be waiting.

Except, there were no children. Just a gang of 6-7 men, mostly undressed. The door shut behind him and he saw the bed. He knew what would happen next.

David saw the tattooed men and instantly knew they were Yakuza, the Japanese mob. He was forced to undress and pose. He was photographed and videoed while he was raped. Each man had his turn and sometimes 2-3 men raped him together. The doctor stood stoically in the corner and watched.

The doctor told him his "tutoring" each week would be serving in the capacity of a child prostitute for the benefit of the Yakuza. If he told ANYONE about this, his parents may be harmed and their reputation in the Japanese community ruined, as the photos and video that had been taken would mysteriously appear at his school and where his parents lived.

So, two to three times per week for nearly two years, David went for his "tutoring" work. He came to think of himself as a prostitute and a whore. He told no one. His clients were Japanese businessmen, foreign businessmen, a smattering of US military officers, a German embassy official and a few wealthy Japanese women. Each time he worked, a Yakuza bodyguard was there to make sure he wasn't harmed too much. Well, as long as it wasn't going to be visually obvious to others, anything was pretty much fair game.

Really, the bodyguard was there to video and photograph. More evidence. More control over David. Another reminder. No one should know. He photographed everything, the sex toys, the bondage, the acts of sexual humiliation like being urinated on or bitten. David said the bodyguard had to intervene on several occasions when things got "out of hand" like the time he was forced underwater and started to struggle.

Then, one day when he knocked on the door at his work, the man answered and told him he was no longer needed. He had become too old. And, the man reminded him what would happen to his family if he ever told of his work.

Much later in life, David realized that many of the videos and photographs taken by his bodyguard may, in fact, still be circulating around the internet. He began to search for them and, in doing so, became addicted to those images he saw, just like me, and was one of the reasons why David was in the same treatment program.

In that Tuesday community meeting when David told his story, you could have heard a pin drop, minus the sobbing of many of us listening. I bowed my head in prayer and begged for forgiveness for the judgment I had placed on David.

David finished by sharing with us that his perfectionism, hyper-awareness and hyper- vigilance grew out of his need for secrecy in protecting his parents. He recognized that it was something that we often judged him for and something he continued to struggle with in his treatment. By acting and being "perfect" he avoided attention and, in his mind, protected the lives of his adoptive parents, two amazing human beings who gave so much to give him love. In fact, he told no one for twenty-five years. His father passed away. He told his mother, after his arrest, separated by the glass in the visiting area of the county jail.

This is a broken, broken world we live in. The men in prison have terrible stories to tell. They weren't just born this way. To make things worse, instead of helping them heal, they are judged and caged and have a really, really hard time earning a second chance outside the razor wire. I hope by hearing David's story, you might think twice before you, too, make any more judgments. That "monster" on the evening news has a story. While nothing excuses the harm we have caused others, let us all think twice about what brought each man to cause that harm.

Yes, God has, and had, me right where he needs me to be. Who am I to question that? There are no coincidences, only God's perfect plan. Trusting Him has truly saved my life.

8 SIMPLE WORDS

I want to wrap up this most important chapter with eight simple words. These are words that have saved my life and words that I will print on a t-shirt one day and wear proudly around town. As I was getting ready to put this chapter together, I kept thinking about II Corinthians 12: 7-10, the passages about Paul's thorn. That idea of strength coming from weakness has come to mean so much to me, especially as it pertains to my new life, my approach to treatment and how I wish to live out the remainder of my life honoring God.

"Therefore, in order to keep me from being conceited, I was given a thorn in my flesh, a messenger of Satan, to torment me. Three times I pleaded with the Lord to take it away from me.

But he said to me, "My grace is sufficient for you, my power is made perfect in weakness." Therefore I will boast all the more gladly about my weaknesses so that Christ's power may rest on me. That is why, for Christ's sake, I delight in weaknesses, in insults, in hardships, in persecutions, in difficulties. For when I am weak, then I am strong." (NIV)

June 25, 2017 was my baptism day. Here, I am surrounded by loves ones as I share my faith story. Then Chanhassen (MN) Mayor Denny can also be seen here. He met with me in prayer regularly after my arrest.

And then my friend Pat and I were walking in the yard one day and I was talking with him about Paul's thorn. He shared with me a message his brother sent him around the time he was sentenced, a message that has really helped him, "Let Go. Let God." They made a lot of sense to me as well.

And so I have combined my own, shortened interpretation of those verses in II Corinthians and the message from Patrick's brother. Together, these eight simple words sum up my faith journey and my healing. They help guide my life each day and I think they can help you too.

BE STRONG. GET WEAK. LET GO. LET GOD.

Pastor Joel Johnson was one of the first people to whom I made a full confession. On December 19, 2016 I met him in his office at Westwood Community Church and gave my life to Christ. Lake Minnetonka was really, really cold this day, but I wasn't having it. My heart was full. I really love this photo.

My heart was full. I really love this photo.love this shirt. That is all.

–2–

PREPARING FOR PRISON

At this point, one of a few things has happened. You may have plead guilty to charges or accepted a plea deal and negotiated a prison sentence via your attorney. The introduction and first two chapters of this handbook were pretty serious in nature. That was for good reason. Still, it is in your best interest to assume the worst in this case. Being mentally and physically prepared for prison is in your best interest. Failing to plan will make your life, and that of your family and loved ones, much more difficult.

This chapter looks at getting your personal things in order before your sentence is executed. Once you are in prison, you will have little contact with outside businesses and it will become very difficult to make purchases, do any banking, file taxes, etc.

BANKING

Start by identifying a *key family member* or trusted friend who is willing to help you while you are gone. In my case, my sister agreed to help me with my banking and taxes. Once you have a trusted person, I suggest you go to your local bank and have that person added to any account you might need to access while in prison. In my sister's case, she also opened her own account there, which made it easy for her to be able to transfer money to/from that account. It may be a good idea to order a small number of checks with both names, in the event there are outstanding bills to be paid. Lastly, leave your debit card with this person and change your bank account address to his/her address as well. That way, any statements, tax documents or new debit cards are sent there.

NAMING A POWER OF ATTORNEY

Another suggestion is to grant a family member or very trusted friend "power of attorney." You can find the paperwork many places online and it will not take long to complete it. Be certain you carefully consider what powers you will grant this person and research the possibilities. Once you have completed the paperwork, you will need to have it notarized. Your bank will be able to do this for you for a small fee.

Securing your important personal documents is also a priority. I recommend either purchasing a small fireproof safe or renting a lock-box at your local bank. Providing a key to a trusted friend or relative is also important, in the event documents are needed while you are away. In the case of a bank security box, you will need to have that person added to the account as well.

The following documents should be placed in secure storage:

❑ Birth certificate

❑ Passport

❑ Social security card

❑ Will

❑ Health care directive

❑ Banking documents

❑ Mortgage/Rental documents

❑ Keys to home and vehicles

❑ Vehicle titles

❑ Credit/Debit cards

In the event you have property you need to store while are you incarcerated, you will need to secure a storage facility or find a friend to store your belongings. If you must rent a facility, know that many facilities will offer a discount if rental storage is prepaid. Save yourself some money!

It is critical to find out if your property is insured by the facility or if you must insure your own property. The same applies if a friend is storing your belongings. Be certain you are covered.

ACCOUNTS AND PASSWORDS

Create a document with your most important account information and passwords. This document should only be shared with a most-trusted friend or relative. I *strongly* advise against giving this to a girlfriend or boyfriend. Boyfriends and girlfriends come and go too often. I have seen too many "Dear John" letters in prison.

The following are examples of account logins and passwords I provided my sister (my power of attorney) before I was sentenced.

❑ Email accounts

❑ Insurance accounts

❑ Student loan accounts

❑ Tax preparation accounts

❑ Bank accounts

RESEARCH PRISON PROGRAMMING

OK, so this is the total geek thing to do, but I found it *so* helpful as I wrapped my head around the fact that I was headed to prison. Do your homework. Find the state's Department of Corrections website and dig around on it.

What should you look for? I learned about the different prisons and their custody levels (more to come on this later), what unique education programs are offered at each site, vocational opportunities available, treatment programs offered, etc. This information was valuable when I first met with my case manager (see page 58).

ADDRESS BOOK

Get a good one, but not a fancy one, not spiral bound and not hardcover. I found a good one on Amazon and filled it. No fewer than a dozen men in prison have offered to pay me a premium for the one I have. Why? The address book they sell here is about the size of my palm.

An address book is on almost every "allowable property" list used at intake. If yours is simple and soft-cover, it will most likely make it through the prison gates.

Focus on names and phone numbers of key support people, as well as prospective employment contacts (in those cases, addresses). I went and got business cards of those in charge of hiring at "felony friendly" businesses and simply taped them into the address book. I was also sure to obtain a card from Human Services in my county, as I wanted to have a contact there to get started on health insurance and financial support, in the event I did not have employment upon release. Lastly, have multiple contact numbers for your attorney.

ALLOWABLE PROPERTY

Obtaining a list of "allowable property" from the state prison system or local jail is absolutely necessary. Too many men and women enter the corrections system without the necessities they are able to take with them. Often, the state system is hard to nail down in terms of what can go with you. I did not find any information on the state website. However, as your first stopping point will most likely be a county jail, the best practice is to contact the person in charge of prison transfers there. They should be more than happy to assist you, as you having <u>only</u> what is allowed helps them to avoid a mountain of paperwork. Remember, they must log every single piece of personal property you bring with you the day of sentencing.....down to the last hairpin, chapstick and penny.

The following list of items were what I was allowed to take with me when I entered prison. These lists are fairly standard nationwide. However, my research indicates there are slight differences. Be sure you get the list for your area.

❏ One pair of prescription glasses—no "readers"

❏ Wedding ring —band only — no diamonds

❏ Address book—soft-cover, no spiral

❏ 20 photos — 4x6, no Polaroid photos with backs. I am guessing you assume this, but no nudity, drugs, guns, etc.

❏ 5 "religious" items — think books, Bible, devotional, etc.

- ❏ Anything related to dentures

- ❏ Money— cash only. I took $1000 to start — realize that the prison may take fees out of this. In Minnesota, that was 20%, because I owed fines. There is *no way* to get around this. Trust me, I tried.

- ❏ Identification —really, just take your driver's license and store the rest in that lock box I encouraged you to get.

- ❏ Medically necessary items —prescription meds, CPAP, etc.

On sentencing day, I had a duffel bag with the above items in it, minus the cash and ID in my pocket. Once I was in my county issued clothes, they took the clothes I wore to sentencing, placed them in my bag and had a family member pick them up. If you don't give them a contact for this, they will dispose of your belongings. It pays to plan ahead, just as you would for a vacation!

SUPPORT SYSTEM

Lastly, and *most importantly*, put your support system together in advance and create an easy way for them to be in contact with one another. This support system will be your lifeline and a means for friends and loved ones to support one another, as well.

This support system should be made up of people who are positive, want you to be well, and people who do not judge you for your crime. They may be disappointed in what you did, but they still love you and want you to be well and succeed. In my case, my support system consisted of family, dearest friends, my girlfriend, people from my church, former colleagues and my attorney.

We decided the most efficient way to keep my support system together was to create a Facebook group. We identified key people to be administrators of the group— namely my girlfriend, children, ex-wife, sister and a couple trusted friends. We made the group private and created a three question process for people to get in the group. Finally, one of the administrators of the group had to approve each member. Members of the group were allowed to invite other members as well.

What did they do in this group? Members were able to share when they spoke with me or heard from me. They could share photos, provide updates on my address, job status, needs, prayer requests, etc. And, when we had visit photos taken by the prison photographer, they were able to post them there too.

Right before my sentencing, my family was able to share my statement for the judge and invite members of the group to my sentencing. By the time I was sentenced, there were approximately 150 members in the group. At sentencing, they had to kick people out because there wasn't enough room in the courtroom. To have that much visible support at that most difficult time was a *huge* boost to me and my children.

Meet my three amazing cherubs (from left to right), Joe, Kate and Tony. I am so proud to be their father and hope they are proud of the man I have become.

Planning ahead for your stay in prison will significantly reduce your anxiety in a time when you and your family will already be stressed enough. Following the simple steps I outlined in this chapter should help ease some of the burden you are already feeling.

Principals aren't always so serious. My daughter Kate helped craft this get-up for a staff development skit at work.

We called this Buca meal "the last supper." On July 25, 2017 we went to dinner as a family unit. My ex-wife Amy, also pictured here, has remained a rock for our children and me. I am so grateful to her for her strength, love, forgiveness and continued friendship.

These three ladies are the best. From left, they are Grammy, my mom and my sister Emily. I felt their love and strength throughout my sentence.
I especially looked forward to Grammy's monthly letters. At age 90, her doctor said she was "amazing" and he was right.

My sister Emily and her husband Lonnie (both standing) joined Kellie and me in the Twin Cities shortly before my sentencing. We did our best to take down the casino buffet and one of us won big at a random slot machine. That person was not me, but will remain nameless. Thank you for sharing and giving me a start on my first canteen order!

It was always aviators with Kellie and me. We traveled to visit my "Grammy" in July 2017. Losing our relationship during my incarceration was one of my greatest tests inside the razor wire. I felt so alone. But, God has ways of making things happen that we do not always understand and that we often need. It is a father's love. Should Kellie and I end up together in the end, we will both be in a better place.

Kellie and I really enjoyed our time together the summer of my sentencing. This was our final dinner together and it remains one of my favorite memories of that time. She was one of the first people to come visit me after my arrest in December 2018 and helped me enjoy my pre-sentencing "bucket list." Eating good food was prominent. Obviously. Just look at my cheeks!

–3–

THE INTAKE PROCESS

Disclaimer:
Before we get into the nuts and bolts of the intake process to the Department of Corrections (DOC), here is a bit of a disclaimer. The first two chapters of this handbook were pretty serious about your trip to prison, preparing for it, etc. And, that was for a good reason.

Now, however, the tone might change just a bit. Mostly, it will change because you need it to. Having some sense of humor while incarcerated is important. You are going to see and hear things that you truly cannot make up. Like people using their hand to stir Kool Aid and claiming that JFK was not assassinated, but actually hidden away for years to mastermind the 9/11 attacks. With Elvis as his accomplice. Also, Tupac is not dead. He and Kurt Cobain are in the house band at the Bellagio.

There is no reason to be alarmed. But, stuff is about to get real.

BOOKING

The intake process will most likely take place the second your sentence is executed. If you are headed to a federal prison, this may or may not be the case. Hopefully, that support system you assembled will be able to be at sentencing and you have lots of hugs and support before you are whisked away.

Very likely, you will be taken into custody at the county jail initially. At this time you will again be booked and photographed. Fingerprints may be needed as well. My rebooking literally took ten minutes, fortunately. Any property you have with you will be inventoried and you will sign for it. At this time, be sure to ask for any religious items you brought and want with you. Just as important, ask for your address book!

Don't get too comfortable in your surroundings, as you will likely be transferred to the intake facility of the DOC in a short period of time. In my case, I waited just 48 hours before I was packed up, shackled and stuffed into the back of a county paddy wagon.

INTAKE FACILITY

Most, if not all, state prison systems have a designated intake facility. How can I put this mildly? You are just a number there. This place will likely be the _very_ worst of all your time in the joint. Once you have completed the orientation process you will likely be transferred again to a more permanent placement.

Of course, all of it depends on your custody level, length of sentence, treatment mandates, etc.

Once you arrive at the DOC intake facility, a welcoming party will await you. They will not be giving hugs, handshakes or offering you Nutty Bars. A-holes. Their job is to process you, fingerprint you, photograph you, assign an offender identification number and badge, strip search you (bend over and smile), weigh and measure you and move you on to the next station. Think like hanging meat in a processing facility, only without the meat hooks.

You will meet very briefly with a health services person to talk medications, mental health, abuse history, medical concerns and the Prison Rape Elimination Act (PREA). The woman who interviews you will talk so fast you can't understand her. Also, she will slur her words because of her tongue-piercing. Well, mine did.

During intake is when they put all of you being processed in a holding pen until all of you have been processed. This is where the bullshit begins. Just keep a low profile. The hardened criminal-types will be posturing and talking "loud." They are simply trying to establish themselves with the corrections officers and other inmates. Don't engage. Let them mark their territory.

Lastly, you will be outfitted with state-issued clothes and given the allowable property you brought with you. Make sure you have what you need.

Brace yourself, the door in front of you is a portal back to the Wild, Wild West. In Minnesota, it is called "E" House, and you will likely hear farm animal noises.

Don't walk with your head down. Look straight ahead. Men may catcall the new recruits, but it will be over as soon as you get your key and cell assignment. Don't expect a single cell unless you have an ass growing out of your forehead. And get used to the idea of a top bunk. I am currently overweight, have had a knee reconstructed and have sleep apnea treated with a CPAP. Never had lower bunk until my final prison destination.

In addition to your orientation, a major goal of your time on "reception" status is to break you down and make you miserable. There are no appetizers at this reception. More than likely you will be locked in your cell for twenty-two hours per day, with one hour for meals and one hour total to shower, make a phone call, grab some ice for soda and, maybe, if you are lucky, catch ten minutes of your favorite television show.

Books, magazines and newspapers now will help you maintain your sanity. Of course, you won't have any library privileges, so have someone coordinate sending you books from Amazon (they must request a gift receipt). I had a subscription to a daily newspaper and I made a lot of friends. I used them to trade for books and puzzle books often. Do crosswords and sudoku -- anything to help you forget about time.

Canteen/commissary will be discussed more at a later point, but I want to emphasize a couple of things here. The second you get your hands on a canteen catalogue, prioritize the following items and get them ordered:

❏ Basic over the counter medications

❏ Hygiene items. The free stuff they give you is horrible.

❏ A few snacks

❏ Condiments

The basic needs are critical in the event you have aches and pains, allergies, etc. *Any* trip to health services will cost you a co-pay. As for those condiments, they will be needed a few times per week when some asshole pulls a stunt and the whole cell house is placed on lock-down status. "Meals on Wheels" (meals delivered to your cell) are horseshit and you will need the condiments to dress up that horseburger they deliver you.

ORIENTATION

The poking, prodding and questioning only scratched the surface at your intake and processing. During orientation, it will be more in-depth. Essentially, the DOC wants to know everything about you, for your own protection and theirs. The following are the major components of your orientation process, which will take you through the first 2–3 weeks.

Handbook orientation— review this informational packet carefully. While some of it is common sense, ignorance is not a valid excuse from the petty rules and regulations

Health screening —you will get a comprehensive physical, including all blood work and testing

Dental exam—unless there are unique circumstances, this will be the last time you see a dentist. Most corrections departments do *not* do routine dental care. Take care of your teeth and pray nothing major happens. Likely, it will not be covered.

Mental health screening— you will see a mental health practitioner and, if needed, a psychiatrist to prescribe medications

Education testing —the DOC wants you to have a diploma. They will require proof of graduation. You may or may not be required to test, if you provide one or if they can verify one. Offenders with a strong educational background are often used as tutors. This is a good job to have.

Chemical dependency assessment— *All* offenders go through this screening. Depending on the results, you may be given a treatment mandate to complete during your incarceration.

CASE MANAGEMENT

The final step in your orientation and reception status will be to meet with your case manager. Remember when I encouraged you to do your homework on all of the prisons in the state and their various programs? That work was for this meeting.

To your case manager, you are one of probably *hundreds* he will see come and go every month or so. They are robots here by design. At your meeting, you will discuss the following:

Custody level and classification

Education

Treatment mandates

Transfers

Recommendations

Q&A

Some things you will want to consider before your meeting. First, use that research you did before sentencing. Ask what prisons you are eligible for, based on your custody level/ points. Next, for what programs might you be eligible? Will you qualify for any early release programs? Is there an application for these programs? Can I apply now? What are the positives and negatives of each of them? What is the likelihood you will be offered treatment before your scheduled release date? Lastly, if you have a preference of which prison, now is the time to verbalize it. The case manager will tell you they have no control over that, but don't believe it. Never assume *anything*. Advocate for yourself.

After you have completed all aspects of your orientation, you will be eligible to transfer to another unit, or if you are extremely lucky, another prison immediately. In Minnesota specifically, you should expect to be in "E" House for 20–40 days. On my 28th day I was moved to "B" House, where I remained for approximately another month. In general, all other houses in St. Cloud have more privileges (library, barber, recreation, etc), though do not forget that you have a few rights in prison. You are at the mercy of the DOC.

-4-

PRISON LIFE

No doubt, this might be the most interesting part of this handbook. And, it is close to the top in the terms of importance. How you live each day will have a significant impact on how well your time in the joint goes. A "lifer" once told me the best way to get along in prison is to "do your own time." That is, remain focused on yourself and do your best to make your time pass without that prison drama and with as much comfort as possible. You, and you alone, have the *most* control over this.

Allow me to make a very direct suggestion to you about prison politicking. Stay out of any conversations about whose crime is worse than others. Take the high road, no matter what you think. All of you, after all, are in prison. It is all bad. Period. Why do I say this? Ranking of crimes, and related conversations, very often leads to extortion attempts and violence. The snowball only gets bigger once you involve yourself in that.

Most likely, sex offenders will be the objects of such talk. I know, as I am serving time for a sex-related offense. The fact I never touched anyone has made it a bit easier on me, but there is still judgment and danger. You will hear offenders discuss "crimes against a person" as being so horrible. I often counter with this question .... Are not all crimes against some person? No one has ever denied it. Get this straight. We have all hurt someone to end up in prison.

If someone asks to see your "papers," do not lie about your crime. Take this chance to take responsibility for what you have done. Often, it will quickly change the tone of the conversation. Ironically, inmates don't like liars.

Remember this always. DO YOUR OWN TIME.

SELF-CARE

My therapists would love that this little section is called "self-care." It is so...... therapeutic. Wait a minute, let me fold my hands, lean back and cross my legs, close my eyes and let the term "self-care" ruminate a bit. Mmmm. There.

Breaking news.... the only person who will care for you in prison is you. You will need to start thinking about small victories and simple pleasures. They will keep you sane. In general, it has been my goal, always in life, to be looking forward to something on my calendar. This is even more important in prison.

Find a calendar for your cell, either from canteen or have someone send it to you via Amazon, if possible. Post it visibly and put everything on it -- birthdays, favorite holidays, next haircut appointment with the prison barber, menu items in the chow hall you don't want to miss, notes to yourself about fun memories on special dates, etc. Do not simply cross off days or do a countdown to release. This will only remind you of your time left, it will not help and will only make things take longer.

Next, accumulate items that remind you of home comforts. Scour the canteen catalogue for things you use in the world -- your preferred soap or hand lotion, shampoo you used as a kid, a snack you and your kids shared together often or a treat your nana always had in that special drawer. One day I passed by the vending machine and saw a big bag of the candied orange slices my kids used to get from their great grandmother -- you know, the ones rolled in sugar that kept them bouncing off the walls all night. The two dollars I spent was a small price to pay for a simple, sweet pleasure that took me to a very happy, loving and warm memory.

No doubt, your cell will be cold and insensitive. Depending on your custody level, the age of the prison, the layout and size of the cell, etc. you will have some opportunity to make where you live your home. And, I suggest you think of this place as your home for awhile. Know the rules for photos and artwork and take advantage of the chance you have to personalize things. For example, Minnesota DOC rules allow for a certain number of "loose" photos, but also allow possession of 40 pages of photos in protector sheets (a photo album). So, on my desk and in my wardrobe I had photos of my kids, my sweetheart, my dog and other close friends. I also created a photo album for my desk. I also cut out and posted sports schedules of my favorite teams.

Prison life is only sedentary if you allow it to be. If you eat and do nothing, you will gain weight rapidly and in large quantities. While your opportunities to be active may be limited, nothing will make you feel worse than doing nothing. Some men choose to bulk up and pump iron. Good for them. I chose to try and be generally healthy, cutting back on food quantity and walking at least once daily. I actually dropped weight in prison. In that way, I was definitely in the minority. In addition to movement in the yard, push-ups, sit-ups and leg raises in your room are generally a good practice.

In the "world," I took for granted how great a haircut, hot shower and shave actually was. Not the case in the "big house." Shower every single chance you get. Please use soap. Shave your face and be *meticulous* about your teeth. One of my "cellies" did not brush his teeth once in the month I lived with him. I offered him toothpaste, to which he responded, "All my teeth are rotten and need to be pulled anyway, so I just quit brushing them." I guess this was an approach I never considered. Don't be this guy. Long story short, the better you care for yourself, the better you will feel about yourself.

Lastly, in terms of self-care, it is of <u>huge</u> benefit to create healthy and productive routines for yourself. Once established, the comfort of knowing what comes next, in a culture of chaos and change, will be very settling to your soul. Early on, I started every single day with a phone call to my sweetheart or other loved one. I built in two periods of time each day to download my emails, listen to music and respond to those emails. This time almost became meditative for me. A lot of days, I ended my evening with a phone call with someone who loved me and cared about me. It made it so much easier to fall asleep in peace.

Again, the *only* person to care for you in prison will be you. Committing to caring for yourself in as many ways as possible should be a big priority.

PRISON STAFF

How can I say this well? Contrary to what other offenders say, you really do need the various officers, case managers, library staff, etc. You will hear inmates say no one should be "talking to cops." But, those dudes are the ones who don't understand the basics of human nature and relationships. There is, however, a delicate line to identify between being a friend to "cops" and being friendly to "cops." After all, it is better the unit sergeant is in your tent pissing out rather than outside pissing in. Duh. You would get wet with some dude's pee.

The key in dealing with prison staff is learning what each one's deal is. We all have a deal. You know, that one thing that we cannot tolerate or drives us nuts? Same goes with any corrections officer. Use prison veterans around you when you are moved to a new prison or unit. Determine who is "by the book," who is close to retirement and doesn't give two shits and who is most respected by the inmates. All critical information. An example? One day I was called to property to pick up some books for my paralegal studies. The property sergeant gave me my books and told me he needed to take the beaded lanyard I wore to hold my ID. Hobby-craft is a "no-no" if you are wearing it. He shared that it was his pet peeve and that, when I got a new one, not to wear it where he works- property, canteen or pill window.

Once you are settled someplace, I suggest you touch base with the chaplain about programming, your case manager about offerings for which you may be eligible, and your unit sergeant and/or lieutenant just because you want them to see you as a person. There are a *lot* of douche-bag, cop-wan-nabe, correction officers. Likewise, there are a lot of very good people who work in prisons and genuinely want you to be well and return to society healthy. Find them.

PRISON FOOD/THE "CHOW" HALL

Let's get the obvious out of the way. You will never have bacon. The hamburger is not really meat. Only on days that end in "z" will you enjoy chicken still on the bone. And never, ever, eat the sloppy joes. The "meat" in them costs the DOC $0.12 per pound. That's a horrifying fact verified by an employee in the kitchen. Canned dog food costs more than that. For real.

It will be hard to be grateful at first, but you will come to be that way. The people in the kitchen try their very best to make food you will enjoy. There is a saying that comes to mind….you can't make an apple pie out of horseshit (well, horse apples). So, dispatch any notion that the food will be good . It won't. Focus on the things that are not "bad" and look forward to them. Put them on that calendar you started.

Understand that a cost effective way for the DOC to keep you full at a reasonable cost is to serve bread with a side of bread and 3oz. of $0.12 per pound "meat." Listen, if you eat all the carbohydrates that you are served you will inflate like the Goodyear blimp. In general, my practice became to skip breakfast and just eat lunch and dinner in the chow hall. Saved calories. If you are lucky, your DOC will also offer an alternate menu at each meal. Think less protein, more carbohydrates and vegetables. Typically, it is also lower calorie. Sometimes, it is the best option. This is where I came to know and love *peanut butter noodles*. Totally gangster. Don't judge.

CANTEEN / COMMISSARY

The canteen catalogue is every offender's treasure. However, it can become a vicious cycle. Just as I said about the "chow hall" you must be very, very careful about what you purchase, cook and eat from the canteen catalogue. Think of it this way. In the world, do you make a monster meal, loaded with carbs and fat, eat it at 9:00pm and then go immediately to bed? No? Then don't start the practice in prison. If you can't say no, no one will recognize you when you walk out the prison door.

The catalogue is filled with snack choices, proteins, pastas, rices, and sweets. Health services will tell you how awful the choices are, but they won't actually take the step of having any changes made to the offerings. Again, I suggest you choose wisely. Don't order on an empty stomach. Calculate how much you will spend <u>before</u> you submit your order. Compare prices in the canteen catalogue to those in the vending machines.

For about $50 per month (not including phone time you purchase), you will be able to live comfortably in the joint. Here are the staples I ordered consistently. This may be a good starting point for you on a weekly basis.

❏ Instant coffee or tea

❏ One bag of hard candy

❏ 1-2 bags chips/crackers

❏ Drink packets (Kool Aid,tea,etc.)

❏ 1 soda

❏ 1 protein

❏ 1 pasta/rice

❏ Prepaid envelopes

More than likely, you will choose to make one meal per week in your cell. The reason? At least once per week, they will serve something inedible in the chow hall. Over time, I also recommend building up your store of condiments. They come in handy when the prison is on lock-down or the mac and cheese needs a little something extra.

Now, a note about "stores." Stores exist in every prison and are run by people to take advantage of you. When your canteen order is delayed or a key product is out of stock, the prices go up- simply supply and demand. Likely, if you are out of coffee and can't wait to receive a bag in your next order, the price will be "1 for 3." That is, dude will give you one bag of coffee and make you sign that you will pay him back three. See where this is heading? Stay away. And, even more importantly, don't run a store yourself. It is a certain trip to the "hole."

"Cooking" is a counterculture in the joint. It has become a "thing" to devise your own special recipe, make it, and then brag about it in the prison. There should be a cooking show on the Food Network about this. It is real science, I tell you. Remember, all you will have to use is a microwave, toaster and some ice. The food in canteen is all processed and refrigeration is not needed. You do the math.

All that being said, it is amazing what some dudes can do with a bag of non-dairy creamer, cocoa powder, and peanut butter. This week, I saw a cheesecake. Last week, the same guy made a pizza. All very impressive, but I think he spent six hours in the kitchenette. Me? I would rather use the time to visit with family, go to the gym or walk outside.

There are 10,000 things you can do with ramen noodles. But the question remains…..why would you want to?

DAY TO DAY COMMUNICATION

No, not with your cellie. Yes, with the modern world. Prisons now are only 5-7 years behind in terms of technology. This means that the U.S. Postal service is still a thing and you still have a mailbox that may contain valuable stuff on a daily basis. Hell, anything in that box is a treat, to be quite honest. Mail means *everything* to someone in prison.

Most, if not all, prisons now allow some form of electronic communication via email, video chat, video messaging and picture messaging. Each system is different and you can bet your ass that someone is reviewing every word and every image. For a price, you will likely be able to order some form of a tablet from an outside vendor. You will plug in and sync that tablet to a kiosk to get your mail, download images, music, etc. Some prisons have wireless capability, which allows offenders to skip the physical process of syncing the device. Of course, emails cost money. However, emails are cheaper than US mail.

Lastly, you will have daily access to the phones, depending on your custody level. The money you spend each month is worth every dime and more. Because of changes to Federal law, telecommunication has become extremely reasonable in prison. Currently, calls are right around 5 cents per minute in most state prisons and some prisons limit the length of calls. In Minnesota, each call can be no more than 15 minutes.

A cost and time saving tip is to have your closest loved ones set up an automatic collect call account with the prison's phone-time vendor. First, it significantly reduces the amount of number-punching for each call. Most importantly, it will likely save some money. In my case, my collect calls are also 5 cents per minute. Because the account is set directly from my bank account, I save the 20% in fees I lose when I transfer money into the prison system, only to add it to phone time. Over your sentence, this may be substantial savings. Twenty dollars saved for every one hundred spent on phone calls is a lot. Twenty dollars equates to six hours and forty minutes of calls!

THE BATHROOM

You deserve to know the truth about using the bathroom in prison. So, I will be blunt about it when necessary. In general, here is a theme you should know. *Always* think of others first when you use the bathroom. Yes, that sounds funny, but prisoners are, for the most part, meticulous about cleanliness and health. Why? Hep C, AIDS, anthrax, polio, cholera, shanghai flu, boogie woogie flu, athlete's foot, hand, foot and mouth disease, etc. Pick one. No one wants it.

You may be fortunate to have a dry cell, which means you will have no running water in your living space. However, it is likely that, at some point, you will have a "wet" cell with a toilet and sink. Close your eyes for a second and think about how fortunate you are to be able to poop and sleep in the same 6x10 space.

Let me pause here and say that most of this section is really designed for the male audience. We are slobs most of the time, so we need reminders. Remember, men, think of others first. What that looks like is the focus of the next couple paragraphs.

Men, you have two options when you need to take a leak. Sit or stand. I will assume you stand all the time, though there is an argument to be made for sitting. Here is the thing, I don't want to step in or sit in your piss dribble. So, when you spray on the seat or accidentally piss-shiver and dribble on the floor, you are going to clean it up when you are finished. Same goes for any other DNA you may leave behind. If you are lucky, there will be a spray bottle in your restrooms with sanitizer. Use it. If you are in a wet cell, use tissue or hand towels.

I have always argued that pooping should be in private. I locked the bathroom door at home and told my kids the only interruption allowed would be for blood, certain death or vomit. Sadly, you need to get over the idea of any pooping in privacy in the joint. You will seldom have a stall door and, if you do, it will be a half door so you can make eye contact with everyone while you crap.

Wet cell or dry, your pooping technique will be the same. Think continuous flush. The second your ass hits the throne, flush. Repeat again and again and again. If you fail to do so, you will have people screaming "put some water on that" at you. The flushing takes care of the embarrassment of any sound and smell you make. You are welcome.

If you share a wet cell with someone else, you can devise a pooping plan together. No joke. It is common courtesy and helps to reduce the anxiety of announcing your bowel schedule. For example, I told my cellie Ken to take his time getting his schizo meds at night so I could poop. When I was gone talking on the phone every night, he did his business. In dorm-style settings, it is often common to stick a toilet card, called a "flag," through your door crack to avoid your cellie walking in while you are on the throne. Don't be embarrassed about making a plan. And, always remember to remove any toilet remnants when you are done. Bacon strips in the bowl are not cool.

A couple other things about bathroom etiquette. You will find no larger collection of homophobes in the world than in a prison. These people would think nothing of peeing immediately next to another man at a stadium piss trough. But, put them in a prison, and peeing immediately next to another man may get your ass beat. Give *lots* of space. If someone is peeing in a urinal and there is an empty urinal next to him, do *not* take that space. Wait your turn or go to the stall to piss. Lastly, angle your body away, as if to shield your groin from any possible sighting. Ridiculous, I know. But, do as I say.

Same rules apply in the shower. More than likely you will be showering with other men at some point. Keep your eyes up. Cover yourself when not showering. Give space. Shower daily. Don't drop the soap. If you do, don't kneel down to get it.

Wear shower shoes *always*. I'll bet you can imagine what things are swishing around on the floor.

Finally, *any* time you use the bathroom, remember to think of others first. Shaving? Clean up any facial hair. Brushing your teeth? No one wants to see your toothpaste spit. Common decency goes a long way in the bighouse. And, you will avoid nasty conflicts by keeping things tidy.

JOBS / EDUCATION / TREATMENT

The very best way to keep your mind off the fact that you are sitting in prison is to be busy. As soon as you are able, apply for a job. Remember, however, you are literally a number to the staff in the joint. You literally wear it everyday. So, it may take extra effort to secure a job. That means you will need to make an effort to find who it is in charge of hiring in each particular area. Write that person to introduce yourself and talk your qualifications and experience. Then, when a job opens, pounce.

Likely, if you do not already have a GED or diploma (and proof of it) you will be required to be in education courses. You will be tested to determine appropriate placement and then placed in your course. In some cases, a "hold" will be placed on you until the time you have completed your degree. In that case, you will not transfer until you are finished. This is an important question to ask your case manager.

Treatment may be a part of your prison sentence. And, you will hear terms like "low, medium or high mandate" thrown around. During intake, you will be assessed for treatment needs. For both sex offender and drug/alcohol treatment, you will be assigned a treatment level. However, don't expect treatment to happen right away, especially if you have a lengthy sentence. I know men who had sentences of 10+ years who did not get treatment until their final two years. And, the possibility exists that, even though you have a mandate, you will not be offered treatment in prison. Instead, you will be required to complete outpatient treatment on the streets.

I have good news and bad news for you. Good news first...... you will be paid in your job. Education and treatment are also considered jobs, so you will be paid for them as well. Here is the bad news. You will likely be paid .25 an hour to start, before fees, fines and gate money are taken out of your paycheck. More about these deductions will be in the chapter called "Finances of Prison."

HEALTH SERVICES

Those who think they know what they are talking about will tell you that you will have the best, free health care while you are in prison. Those people are dumb. You have access to healthcare, yes. However, every visit is a fight for what you need. One of the men in my treatment program was in hour 48 of heart failure before someone finally came to his senses and ordered him to the hospital. Then the conversation revolved around who would pay for the ambulance ride.

What you get for help comes down to money. If the DOC can fix something for a $2 pill, that will be the solution until the situation gets so bad, they are left with no other choice than to pay for it. The best example I can give you of this is in the area of dental care. In Minnesota, you cannot get your teeth cleaned until you have served a minimum of 36 months and have at least another 8 months left on your sentence. The *only* time you will be seen by a dentist is when it is too late: an excruciating cavity, an abscess or an infection. Then, they *may* fill it. But, because they won't do root canals in prison, you will be offered a root canal at your own cost or they will pull your tooth at no cost.

Bottom line, do your *very* best to care for yourself in the joint. Have over-the-counter meds in your cell, brush and floss your teeth daily, get exercise and do your best to eat well. The last thing you want is to have to depend on the DOC to keep you alive.

PRISON POLITICS

Listen. I said it before and I will say it again here. Prison is one big Jerry Springer episode. Don't watch it. Don't get on stage. There are gangs. Extortion happens. People fight and talk big. Stay away.

The path to a drama-free prison stay is plowed by you. Do your own time. Period.

PRISON SURVIVAL TIPS

If making your time easier sounds like it might be a great idea, here are some recommendations from seasoned prison vets for improving your day-to-day prison life.

- If you have a television, subscribe to a television programming guide of some type. Regular mail feels good and, surprise, there are no DVRs in prison.

- Skip the extra carbs at each meal. You don't need the bread with the turkey ala king over biscuits.

- Get into puzzles, crosswords, word searches and Sudoku.

- At every single opportunity, get outside for fresh air.

- Friend a "lifer" and ask him for tips or what has made his/her life easiest in prison.

- Get to know the unit swamper. He or she has access to a lot of goodies like tape, rags, click pens, paper clips, paper and such in and around the officers' desk. For a scoop of coffee or a ramen noodle, you can acquire a lot.

- Pick up a new hobby or game. Ever played handball? It is THE prison yard game. Beading, knitting, crotchet and drawing and painting are all HUGE in prison. Pass your time by making gifts for your friends and loved ones.

- Utilize the Inmate Magazine Service (have a support person look it up online). For around $40 you can get TEN magazine subscriptions to major magazines you like to read. When you are done reading them, remove your address label and use them to barter for things you need.

- Your dessert at chow, Ramen noodles and Tide Pods are all forms of currency in prison.

- Do NOT count down your days to release. Instead, Do think of milestones. For example, only two Thanksgivings left. It feels like less.

- Buy the shower shoes, no matter the cost. Same with nail clippers. NEVER loan them out.

- ALWAYS have a mixture of condiments on hand.

- ALWAYS assume canteen will be closed unexpectedly. Keep extras of hygiene, coffee and popcorn in your bin, tucked away safely.

- Never, EVER conduct a business transaction with anyone in prison.

- Express gratitude outwardly every single day. Be grateful for the extra fries, the kind approach of an officer and the extra envelope that was mistakenly placed in your canteen bag.

IMPORTANT CANTEEN ITEMS TO HAVE ON HAND

- Cream cheese is a must if you can get it. Ours was jalapeño flavor. Used it in queso, mac and cheese and for making chip dip.

- Buy any type of salsa offered. I added it to that same queso and put it in my chili recipe. Salsa has a whole mess of seasonings in it that are otherwise not available on the canteen menu.

- Pasta sauce, for all of the same reasons you want salsa on hand. Seasonings, plus it will act as a thickener in other sauces. It has tomato paste in it.

- Macaroni and cheese is a must. Use the powder as a base for a thickener when you make cheese sauce for your nachos.

- A backup toothbrush and shampoo. You will forget the shampoo at least once per year and leave it in the shower. Some thirsty jackass will take it and you will never see it again.

- Ramen. Because it is ramen. Seasoning packets go well on popcorn or in that chili or mac and cheese. The noodles can always be used as filler.

- Always, always, always keep ibuprofen and some other pain killer on hand. If you go to Health Services, they will charge you good money for two of them. The whole bottle will cost you less than $2.

- Must have squeeze cheese. It goes in everything you will make.

- Any condiments you can afford. Prison food is no treat.

- Coffee. As much as it may hurt the pocketbook, buy the good stuff if you have two choices. In prison, Folgers tastes like that large dark roast you used to buy on the streets.

TEN QUICK WAYS TO GET SENT TO THE "HOLE"

The only good thing about being in segregation is the single cell. Otherwise, you get one phone call per week and one hour per day out of your room. The food is cold, as are the showers. And, you don't have any visiting privileges while you are in the "hole." Unless all those things sound appealing to you, best to avoid the following situations:

1. Alter a razor in ANY way. Do not break off the handle or the razor head. Only dispose the razor in the provided sharps containers.

2. Be in an "unauthorized area." This means even just taking the long way back from the property building.

3. Make a "pass" or anything that may be interpreted as a "pass" at a DOC employee or officer. This includes asking an officer anything personal about her/him, such as family.

4. Deny your room placement because you don't like your "cellie."

5. Possess anything that may be construed as "escape materials." One guy in our unit had an extra sheet and pillow case in his room. Never saw him again. Shipped out for possessing "escape materials." Also, don't ask anyone to send you any kind of map. Not a good idea.

6. Fail to follow an officer's directive. Even if the officer is wrong and you fail to do it, buh-bye. If there is not a specific rule about something, whatever the officer says instantly becomes that missing rule. Deal with it.

7. Get too "handsy" in the visiting room. The visiting room is no joke. Don't mess it up.

8. A fight, horseplay or any type of physical contact with another inmate.

9. How do I say this? Well, there is no other way but to be direct. Don't get caught masturbating.

10. Not having the EXACT proper pill count for your KOP meds or combining any type of meds into a bottle that is not properly labeled. I saw a guy go to the "hole" for combining two bottles of ibuprofen into the same bottle. This is a major offense, as ridiculous as that might see.

–5–

QUIPS

YOU KNOW YOU'RE IN PRISON WHEN...

- you cannot be trusted with the stick from your corn dog.

- BM stands for "Baby Mama."

- you have eaten a steak purchased from a vending machine.

- you may be falling in love with a woman named Cactus Annie (please Google this)

- you can use a spork like a ninja.

- cleaning the "house" takes less than ten minutes.

- your day revolves around the bathroom schedule of another man.

- you start to believe that those Golden Corral commercials look pretty good and that piece of shoe leather you once had at Ponderosa maybe wasn't that bad after all.

- you forgot about zippers

- you know a guy who once loved Ozzie Osbourne so much that he tattooed his name on his knuckles.

- you tear cologne/perfume ads out of magazines and slather your body with them just so you can smell like a man/woman again.

- the first thing you do when you get your "clean" linens is shake them out and remove another man's pubic hair. And, you are grateful for that fact that those pubic hairs you found on your "clean" linens had at least been washed.

PRISON HACKS TO KNOW

- Always save your microwave popcorn bag. It can be used to "fry" things.

- Run your popcorn under water before you microwave it. Just one quick run through the water. Just try it. Better corn.

- Nacho chip bags can be pulled apart, wiped out and used as wax paper. This was my hack when I made peanut brittle.

- Any toothpaste with peroxide or whitener in it makes a wonderful stain remover.

- Save containers and bags you get with the meals on wheels.

- Never give up your shoelaces when you turn in a pair of shoes. They make great drawstrings in oversized pants and shorts.

- As someone approaches release, find out what they are not taking with them. Most often, they will give up their prison issue jeans and sweats, as well as plastic containers, leftover hygiene products, etc. Be sure you also pay it forward before your release.

6

THE FINANCES OF PRISON

Let's get one thing straight from the outset. The DOC in your state is not set up to lose money. It is a business just like any other. As such, the DOC will nickel and dime you and your family, as well as the taxpayers at large, to squeeze out every single dollar it can. It behooves you to know the various systems and fees you will encounter while incarcerated.

Before I get into the various fees and accounts set up in the Minnesota DOC, let me again emphasize that you carefully read the offender handbook given to you during the intake process. It will contain important information about the accounting system in prison. I also suggest you buy a manila envelope or plastic accordion file from canteen right away. In it place *every* single receipt and financial transaction statement you receive. This is for your own protection.

ACCOUNTS | The DOC will set up a variety of accounts for you once you are in the system. Again, check the offender handbook to be sure you understand, and can easily track where your money is going.

SPENDING | This is your primary account and be compared to your personal checkbook on the streets. From this bucket, you will purchase canteen, order from DOC approved vendors, send money to family or your bank via a voucher, etc. If you need to use Health Services for anything, your co-pay will be withdrawn from your spending account.

GATE (SAVINGS) | The DOC does not want you to go through the exit without some money in your hand. So, during your stay, it will collect dollars via the GATE fee (discussed later) to send with you when you leave. In Minnesota, you are guaranteed to leave with a minimum of $100, even if the DOC must gift it to you. The maximum amount of money you can accumulate in MN in your gate is $500. Upon release, you are given a prepaid credit card with your GATE savings loaded on to it.

FINES | Unless you paid your fines in full at sentencing (or you are fortunate enough to not have fines), the DOC will take money to pay your fines and place it in a separate account.

SAVINGS ACCOUNT | Once your fines and GATE savings are paid up in full, you will likely have the option of transferring money into a DOC savings account that offers interest.

FEES | In addition to the money that the DOC gets from taxpayers through taxes, other government entities for treatment and the Federal government, it will want to collect more money from you and your family. The DOC does this through various fees. Primarily, there are four categories.

COST OF CONFINEMENT | This is the largest fee you will face in the joint. In my experience, the cost of confinement fee applied to every dollar transferred into my spending account. That meant that 10% was deducted from every deposit I personally made or a loved one made. Bringing in $1,000 with you to start your sentence? The first $100 goes to the DOC. Your nana sent you $10 of her social security check for your birthday? They get the first dollar.

FINES | Of any of the fees, this one makes the most sense in my opinion. You have an obligation to pay for your fines. So, until those fines are paid, the DOC will take an additional 10% from any dollars placed into your spending account. Note, until your fines are paid in full, that means 20% of any money deposited into your account will be taken from you.

CANTEEN | In my experience, an additional 5% was tacked onto every canteen purchase until my fine was paid. This was in addition to local taxes. So, $100 in Ramen and Chick-O sticks costs you $105.

GATE FEE | As referenced earlier, the DOC wants you to have money when you are released. Makes sense. As a result, they will take from you until the fee has been paid. In Minnesota, this money is collected through your paycheck (if you have a job). I was charged at a rate of 50% until my fee was collected. If my paycheck for 60 hours was $15 (yes, that is correct), $7.50 was taken for my GATE fee and my final paycheck for two weeks was $7.50.

BUDGETING

Start your planning now before you walk through those prison doors. If you struggle with finances in the "world," you are going to learn very fast about them in the joint. Technically, the DOC will tell you that you have no need for money in prison. Can you live without it? I guess so, but that means no phone calls, the indigent supplies they provide (soap, toothpaste, a toothbrush, basic hygiene, a couple envelopes, etc.) and chow hall food only. If you have the means, plan for $50 per month spending (in addition to phone time).

If you can make it happen financially, plan to purchase the following as soon as you are able. These items will help you with your time immensely.

- ❑ Fan–$25–not many prisons have AC. Worth every penny.

- ❑ Television–$175–$250. The DOC does provide a lot of television programming. Note: there are no personal TVs allowed in the Federal system currently.

- ❑ Tablet–$60–$150, for email, music and games. Emails are around $.40 per "stamp" and most songs run $1.29-$1.99 and games average $8-$10.

You will likely have the opportunity to earn income in prison, though it may take a while for that to happen. In prison, jobs, education, and treatment are all paid positions. Provided you are full-time, approximately 30 hours per week, you can safely budget that you will have $20–$30 per month in net income (after fees).

My suggestion would be to set aside your monthly income for phone time and media (songs, games, etc.). Then, you will only need money for snacks, preferred hygiene items, envelopes, etc. Lastly, do not forget to calculate your fees into your budget. The DOC is taking them whether you like it or not.

Please note that every state prison system is different, as is the federal system. What I have shared is based on some research and my personal experience. Use your time in the cell to read your prison system's financial policies and fees carefully, just as you would any other financial document. Your money is a precious commodity in the joint. Protect it.

7

SUPPORT SYSTEMS

The only way the offender and his/her loved ones will make it through the time before them is with a strong network of support. This network does not need to have a lot of bells and whistles, but it should be created, connected and planned before sentencing, if at all possible. Two support systems need to exist, one for loved ones and one for the offender. And, they should work together and feed one another.

RELATIONSHIPS WHILE INCARCERATED

I struggled with where to appropriately place this section on relationships. Honestly, I thought my long-standing relationship could stand the test of time. As I write, I am no longer convinced of this, though only God knows the plans He has in store for me and my girlfriend, friend, whatever we are at this moment in time. This next point deserves its own paragraph because you need to let this sink in.

It takes an exceptionally special kind of man or woman to "do time" with their loved one. Think one in 5,000 kind of man or woman.

Why is this? Because your incarcerated life, for you, is a stop in time. Your loved one must continue to live in the world—a world full of wants, needs and temptations. And, you must understand the loneliness he/she feels while you are gone.

As a newbie to the prison life, boy was I naive. There are three approaches to relationships while incarcerated.

1. Break it off—do your time and, if it is right, it will still be love in the end.

2. Don't ask, don't tell—it is what it is. This approach is the most popular, the motto being "as long as he/she still takes my calls, writes, visits, supports and meets me at the door when I get out, nothing else matters." But, you must let go of any control and trust in this scenario.

3. Carry on in a committed relationship—yes, it can happen; no, it will not be easy. There are men in my unit whose spouses have remained with them over ten years. It is possible.

Regardless of your feelings as you approach your sentence, the most important thing to remember is that communication is number one. Feelings may change -- stronger or weaker. Be realistic. Remember we all make mistakes. Life alone, in prison or in the world, is extremely difficult.

SUPPORT FOR YOUR LOVED ONES

I am intentionally placing this section first because, quite frankly, it is by our actions that our family and loved ones are without us. It is upon us to care for them and support them by any and all means possible.

My family and friends receive a weekly letter from me, a letter I commit to writing every Saturday. It is not overly long, but does give some insight into my daily life, my struggles and anxieties and any general news updates. I send it to a dear friend who scans it and emails it to a designated email group. In addition, he agreed to post some summary of the information to the Facebook group we created. More than a few people have indicated the information shared weekly is extremely helpful to them.

While you are gone to the joint, you will likely have a lot of personal items going unused—a car, technology, furniture, household items, etc. Find someone to use them during your absence. Don't worry, they will give it back when you are out. Loaning these things out serves two purposes. One, it leaves a part of you with the loved one. Two, it probably helps the person out. Your kids will love drinking their favorite beverage out of their father's favorite coffee mug... you know, the mug you have washed twice in the past year.

One thing that will weigh on you, as it has me, is that being in prison means you will likely struggle with financial support of your family. If at *all* possible, leave some money with a trusted friend for special occasions—birthdays, holidays, etc. I prepaid an Amazon Prime account and gave a loved one access so gifts could easily be shipped to my kids. A favorite of theirs so far was when I sent a treat of peanuts and candy corn with a sweet note for Halloween—something we always had in the house at that time of year as a family.

Before my sentencing I also pre-made meals and froze them for my family and my girlfriend. So, for some time at least, they had meals prepared to help them amongst all of their own chaos. Selfishly, it also provided comfort to me knowing I had been able to provide in some way.

Another recommendation is to help your loved ones find professional resources in advance of your absence, be it a therapist or counselor or simply a list of resources available to the families of incarcerated men and women. A good place to start is your local churches, service organizations and social services. In addition, I solicited a close knit network of friends and family to be a support team for my family and girlfriend. Often times, they simply check in and chat. Other times, they help with an oil change on the snowblower or a gift card to the grocery store. They know how much their support of my loved ones helps support me.

Lastly, and most importantly, your calls and emails mean everything to your loved ones. I found it helpful to create a pretty strict routine of calls each week to family. Then, I mixed in a rotation of emails and calls each week to other friends and loved ones as I was able. In the grand scheme of things, a forty cent email or fifty cent phone call is a small price to pay—much more important than that extra package of ramen noodles or the bag of Cactus Annie nacho chips.

One more thing is important to emphasize about communicating with your loved ones. Talk about your release like it is tomorrow. Plan that first meal together, talk about clothes you want in the car for changing into and ask your loved ones to visualize that day and time. I found it provided us so <u>much</u> hope.

SUPPORT FOR THE INMATE

Let's start with the fact you are seeking information via this handbook —this is means of support already. Very soon, if he or she has not already, your loved one will realize that you are serving a sentence as well. The fact that you are standing by him or her, even as you also suffer the consequences, says so much about your love and strength. And that is an inspiration.

Without a doubt, the single most supportive and amazing thing you can do is remain in communication by *any* means possible. So many men and women are forgotten and serve their sentences in isolation. Nearly every prison now has some form of electronic communication available to inmates. Some, in fact, even have devices available for texting, though the costs for that are ridiculous and damned close to extortion. An email in that inbox or a letter mailed to the offender is an instant game-changer. Before my incarceration, I thought that sounded silly, but I don't now. I know what it feels like to open that mailbox and see something there.... I am not forgotten.

Technology also allows you to send photos and videograms. Obviously there are pretty strict requirements on them but, unless you send something that clearly violates those rules, you will not have problems. I get to see photos of my kids, my family, my golden retriever, and all those special occasions I am missing with them. My favorite, however, is the videograms —seeing my son play hockey, getting a tour of my kids' new apartment, watching my kids open their Christmas or birthday gifts or just seeing my dog playing with his favorite chew toy. I watch them over and over again.

Depending on your loved one's custody classification and facility, you will be able to visit either in person (contact visits) or via video chat (non-contact visits). Each facility has its own rules for getting on the offenders visiting list and visiting. My advice is this..... Read them very, very carefully. I have had people rejected for using the last version of a form, for forgetting to sign the form and for having an out of date address. When it says to use black pen only, follow the instructions. Sadly, the DOC likes to make it difficult in any circumstance it can. This most certainly includes visiting.

Familiarize yourself with the visiting rules completely. You will be turned away if you violate, in even the slightest way, the rules on dress code, contact during visits, feet being on the floor, etc. And, if you get on the DOC's list for violating the rules, the consequences are terribly severe for both you and your loved one.

I have often been asked by my support network about sending money. Often, I tell them it is a kind offer and not necessary because I do not want to be a burden. However, I will admit here that every penny means so much and that I often pray at night for God to provide me financial support. Without money, little happens in prison. Phone calls are not made, emails not sent, snacks not purchased. Can you survive without money in prison? Technically, yes. But it ain't easy.

That being said, there are other ways to financially support without sending money directly. Consider funding media purchases for music and sending emails or providing financial assistance for correspondence courses. Another option might be purchasing a periodical subscription or sending books from an online seller. Books, magazines, and newspapers are a hot commodity in the joint, commodities that can be traded for snacks, pre-paid envelopes or Kool-Aid mix. Finally, you may choose to set up a prepaid collect call account so that your incarcerated friend or family member can call you at no cost to him/her. As I have shared previously, collect calls are pretty cheap if you keep a prepaid account with the prison's phone service provider.

Another type of support you might consider is connecting your loved one with resources on the outside. Prison case managers have hundreds of men on their caseload and a limited amount of time to spend on each one. This is a sad reality. Any work you can do on behalf of your friend in advance of release will help the whole process. Parole agents are also very busy and the more support an offender has upon release, the less time he or she will need to spend "chasing" the offender around. With a lot of support, and a solid release plan, the offender will likely have far fewer release conditions. And, most importantly, the research shows that a strong support network significantly reduces recidivism rates.

As I suggested earlier, talk about that release date like it is tomorrow. Hope. A common phrase for me with my support network has been "I can't wait." Hold on to those positive thoughts, make release plans and be positive. Always.

From L-R, meet the "three amigos," Scott, Dave and Mark. These men stood by me from beginning to end and taught me so much about humility, gratitude, grace, and God's relentless love. On this scorching summer day, they moved the last of my things into storage.

Meet "Party in a Box." Shane (front), Eric (back left) and Steve are my best buddies from high school. They stood by me at my lowest and supported me during my recovery. Really, we can make anything fun together. This night, we enjoyed one last opportunity to hang out in Minneapolis, devour wings, laugh and take over the jukebox. Just like always.

–8–

COPING TOOLS

WORSHIP PLAYLIST RECOMMENDATIONS

The following songs were the core of my worship playlist. The longer I was in prison, the more important this playlist became to me. I wish I had had it from the very first day and I hope you find some songs you like.

The Secret Place
(featuring Madison Cunningham) by Phil Wickham

Broken Things by Matthew West

Lord I Need You by Matt Maher

Your Love Never Fails by Jesus Culture

Reckless Love by Cory Asbury

Love Like This by Lauren Daigle

How He Loves by David Crowder Band

How Great is Our God by Chris Tomlin

What a Beautiful Name by Hillsong Worship

Sinking Deep by Hillsong Young and Free

To My Knees by Hillsong Young and Free

All My Hope by Crowder

Out of Hiding by Steffany Gretzinger

Who You Say I Am by Hillsong Worship

Something Beautiful by NEEDTOBREATHE

Love Will Always Win (Studio Version) by Travis Greene

So Will I (100 Billion X) by Hillsong United

Stand in Your Love by Bethel Music and Josh Baldwin

Whom Shall I Fear (God of Angel Armies) by Chris Tomlin

You Say by Lauren Daigle

He is Jesus by North Point InsideOut and Seth Condrey

Undignified by David Crowder Band

Meant to live by Switchfoot

Red Letters by Crowder

Brother by NEEDTOBREATHE

Survivor - Live from Harding Prison by Zach Williams
(whole CD)

FIVE BOOKS TO READ OVER AND OVER AGAIN
1. The Case for Grace by Lee Strobel
2. Love Does by Bob Goff
3. The Shack by William Paul Young
4. Purpose Driven Life by Rick Warren
5. The Bible

HOPE. FAITH. LOVE.
SCRIPTURE PASSAGES TO INSTANTLY LIFT YOUR SPIRITS

- Jeremiah 29:11-14
- Galatians 5:1
- Il Corinthians 13:4-13
- Romans 8:28-39
- II Corinthians 12: 7-10
- Matthew 6:25-34
- Isaiah 59
- Luke 15:32
- Acts 9: 17-18
- Romans 6: 6-7
- John 8: 12
- Romans 12: 1-2
- Philippians 4: 4-9
- Hebrews 13: 5-6
- Micah 6:8
- Matthew 22:36-40
- Ephesians 4:32
- Titus 3: 5-6
- Psalms 19: 7-11
- Joshua 1: 1-9

A FINAL THOUGHT

Just weeks before my sentencing, I traveled to visit my 88-year-old grandmother at her log cabin nestled in the Hiawatha National Forest. I went for two reasons—one was to tell her about my offense and pending prison time (she knew nothing). It was emotional, to say the least. Second, as I was facing sitting in prison for 40 months, I was afraid she might be gone before my release.

Not surprisingly, she was a rock. I cried when she asked if I had forgiven myself. Worse, I bawled as I was readying to leave that last day. I intended to say goodbye, probably forever. She gave me the biggest, most amazing Grammy hug and said with such confidence, "Tim, I am not going to tell you goodbye. I will see you later."

Please remember those wise words of my grandmother.

GLOSSARY

bird bath:
a term used by inmates to essentially describe bathing in one's cell in the sink. "Dude pissed in the shower so I will be taking a bird bath until the swampers scrub the hell out of it."

bit/bid:
a prison sentence that is served. "My first bit was seven years for aggravated burglary."

BM:
you might think bowel movement, but that is just wrong. In prison, your BM is your baby mama, i.e. the mother of your child. Classy right? "My baby mama (BM) is coming to visit."

books:
essentially, a prison savings or spending account. "My mom just put twenty dollars on my books."

canteen:
the place where you pick up your canteen order or a reference to what you will be ordering or have already ordered. Some prisons also call this commissary. "I got a 140 bag coming from canteen next week."

case:
in prison, this is a very specific reference to someone who has a sex-related case. "I heard dude has a case."

case manager:
essentially, your high school guidance counselor, but for prison. Can be immensely helpful or totally worthless. Pray for a good one. "My case manager sent me a pass to see him after chow."

cellie: your cellmate. "My cellie is a real jerk."

cheek:
to smuggle your prescription pills in your cheek, only to sell them to someone else. "He cheeks his 'wellies' (wellbutrin) at the pill window." Do realize that, if you decide to purchase said cheeked pills, they are coming from dude's mouth and you will likely also get his Hep C and HIV. You are warned.

cho mo:
prison slang for a child molester or someone who has "a case." Sometimes this is shortened to just "cho."

choppin' it up:
means having a conversation. "Dude and me were choppin' it up when they called count."

chow:
generic term for any prison meal. "Are you going to chow this morning?"

CO:
corrections officer generally. There are different ranks such as sergeant, lieutenant, commander, etc.

come up:
a sudden increase in funds on your books.

contact visit:
a visit that allows contact such as a hug, kiss on the cheek, handshake, etc. as your visitor enters and exits.

count:
the process by which offenders are counted each day. This usually takes place 3-4 times per day, more at higher custody level prisons. "Standing ID count will begin in two minutes."

crib: home

custody classification:
the level of custody by which you are imprisoned. In Minnesota, the custody classifications are super maximum, maximum, medium and minimum.

dap:
two inmates bumping fists together in lieu of a handshake.

day space:
a common area where offenders can gather during the day to watch television, play cards, etc. "Switch in, the day space is now closed."

dead time:
the time you must spend in confinement before you complete your treatment mandate or are released. For those inmates with no treatment mandate, it is all dead time.

dinner sausage:
a trumped up, garbage name for hot dog that the nutritionist uses on the menu to disguise the fact that you are eating pro-

cessed turkey beaks, lips and assholes. Offenders also refer to it as the homewrecker. This is on the menu at a women's prison, they call it "ladies night".

DOC:

Department of Corrections- the department everyone in the world thinks protects them from monsters until they are reformed. Except, they seldom correct a damned thing. Don't believe the hype.

drop a kite:

to snitch in written form.

ECRC:

acronym for End of Confinement Release Committee. For any felonies that require predatory offender registration, you may go before this committee to find out your level of release. In Minnesota, the levels are I, II or III. In general, you want to go to the hearing if you wish to try and have your level reduced. This generally takes place 4-6 months before your SRD/MRD.

fire:

an adjective used to describe something amazing, most often food. "That pineapple cake tonight was fire."

flag:

It is the prison term for a recreation period, recreation used loosely. Generally, you will get an hour or two of FLAG to shower, use phones, check email, etc. per day. This term is more commonly used in higher level custody prisons. "Galley 84, doors open for FLAG." Note, a second definition. The piece of paper you stick out your cell door to keep others away while you poop. "I can't get in my cell right now. My cellie has the flag out."

galley:
a number assigned to a tier of cells. Generally, odd galleys are on one cell block and even are on the other.

GATE Fee:
also called your GATE. This is money collected from your wages and deposited dollars that you get upon release. The DOC doesn't want you to leave without money to get your life restarted. In Minnesota, the minimum GATE Fee is $100 and the maximum is $500.

HOF:
an acronym for Housed Out of Facility. Prison systems that are overfull will often contract with county jails for space. If you are one of the unfortunate souls who gets placed "HOF," do everything in your power to get moved back to a DOC facility. The county jails are generally horrible places to do "dead" time.

hole:
also known as "SEG" or segregation. You don't want to do anything that gets you sent to the hole. You will have very little contact with anyone for long periods at a time. It is a disciplinary place.

hood books:
urban fiction, a *very* popular literary genre with inmates.

hot:
a term used to describe the increased possibility of disciplinary actions, especially due to an increased CO presence. "Make sure

you lock your foot locker, it is awful hot in the unit lately."

hug rug:
the designated mat or rug in the visiting room where offenders are to greet their visitors and hug (five seconds only), shake hands, give a peck on the cheek, etc.

hustlin':
effort to exchange goods or services for a profit.

house:
to hide something in your groin area for the purpose of smuggling contraband. For example, I once saw a dude "house" an empty chip bag from the chow hall. He claimed empty chip bags work well for "frying" things in the microwave...things to include the short and curlies in the chip bag from such "housing." Hurl.

HRU:
stands for Hearings and Release Unit. If a person comes back to prison on a violation (see RV), she/he often goes before HRU for a hearing to determine how long the violation stay will be. If your return to prison requires completion of a treatment mandate before release, you will likely be assigned something like "180 days or less."

ICS: acronym for "Incident Command System." A fight would initiate an ICS and all offenders would be sent back to cells until it had been properly dealt with and investigated. Warning... an ICS brings out mace and dogs that will try to eat you. No good. "All offender movement has stopped for an ICS."

indigent:
a status for offenders who have no money on their "books."
Indigent offenders can order basic hygiene and over-the-counter
items weekly from canteen on the DOC's dime. You want to read
indigent rules carefully to see if you qualify.

Inmate.com:
this is the rumor mill in prison. "I heard via inmate.com that we
are getting new satellite television service on Tuesday." Only in
days that end in "Z" should you believe anything you hear from
this news source.

IR:
acronym for investigative restriction. If you accuse someone, or
are accused, of a minor violation you may be placed on IR while
an investigation is conducted. Minor violations, such as assault,
lead directly to the "hole." "Dude accused him of stealing some
noodles, so he is on IR."

janky:
of poor condition.

kiester:
in the words of that hilarious and classic "Newlywed Game"
clip (find it), "that would be up the butt, Bob." In other words, to
hide something in one's anal cavity for the purpose of smuggling
contraband. Any of the drugs that make it into a prison were
in a person's ass at some point. Let that be your warning. "He
kiestered some weed on the way in."

kite:
the primary means of internal communication in the prison

system. Essentially, it is a form of you use to send questions to your case manager, therapist, health services, etc. It is no coincidence it is called a kite. Remember kites as a kid? Sometimes they flew just fine, others they crashed and burned or were torn to shreds and, sometimes, they were lost forever. Yep, just like that. "Send a kite to the chaplain for a list of service times."

kite out:
beg for movement out of a unit.

KOP:
acronym for "keep on person." Medications you are allowed to keep on person in your cell. If you are on basic meds for cholesterol, anxiety, asthma, etc. you will likely house them in KOP (they are accounted for carefully). "My inhaler is KOP."

lifer:
someone who is serving a life sentence. "Dude killed someone. He is a lifer."

lock-down:
a status in a housing unit. It sucks. Generally, a lockdown comes as a result of an ICS, which you hopefully already read about. You won't be out of your cell if your unit is on lock-down status.

LOP:
acronym for "loss of privileges." A form of informal discipline for smaller infractions such as not making your bed, maintaining a messy cell, bringing food back from the chow hall, etc. If you are on LOP, you cannot be in day rooms, use the phone, check email, use the gym or yard, etc. "Dude got two days LOP for failing to lock his foot locker."

mandate:
directed requirement given by your case manager, agent or judge. Most often, a mandate is given for necessary treatment and will sometimes be assigned a low, medium or high priority. Just because you have a treatment mandate does not mean you will be given treatment in prison. You may be required to complete outpatient treatment upon release.

MRD:
mandatory release date. Generally, this is the date at which the DOC literally no longer has any say over you. It is the expiration of all of your time, the prison sentence and any parole or conditional release time you have remaining.

non-contact visit:
a visit where no physical contact is allowed, likely conducted via video or through glass with a phone. Broadly, violent offenders, sex offenders, and those serving time in "seg" are offered non-contact visits if they have such restrictions. "You can only have non-contact visits with your minor son/daughter."

old-school:
an older man in prison. This is a term of endearment for those of us over the age of 40. "Hey, old-school, what's good?"

papers:
the paperwork provided to you by the court and/or your case manager that names your offense and custody points, classification and sentence. If someone wants to see your "papers" they are trying to determine your crime. Don't show them; just be honest.

OG:

old-ass gangster or old guy. This is a term of affection, much like "old school."

PRD/DRD:

projected or discretionary release date. For "RVs," this is the date they are projected to complete treatment and/or be released.

PREA:

acronym for the Prison Rape Elimination Act. Accuse someone of a PREA violation and alarm bells will go off, you will be put on investigative restrictions(IR) and confined to your cell until an investigation is completed. This is a serious allegation. Some advice.... stay away from any sexual jokes or behaviors in the joint. "That is some PREA shit."

Prison purse:

Ummmmm. Well, you know. Your butt. "That dope got through the gate in his prison purse."

pump your brakes:
slow down a minute

rack: $1000.
"Dude got ten racks for that car."

RV:

is Release Violator, someone who was out in the world and screwed up and is now back amongst the incarcerated. Usually, these violations are not new crimes, but violations of the terms of a person's release. An example would be using a controlled substance, not reporting an address change, leaving the state without permission, etc.

salty:
really irritated

sellin' woof tickets:
talking smack over the galley

SHU:
pronounced like "shoe," this is an acronym for "short-term housing unit." Living in the SHU sucks because it is where all the parole violators and disciplinary issues live. You will have limited privileges there and it will be much like the place you lived during intake. Stay away.

sketchy:
not to be trusted.

smash:
don't run for cover, as this is not something you do to someone. Rather, you most often do this to your favorite food. In prison, it means to eat it all, enthusiastically. "Man, I'm gonna smash these nachos tonight during the game."

SO:
acronym for sex offender. "He must complete SO treatment."

SRD:
acronym for "supervised release date." "What is your SRD?"

swamper:
sometimes also called "house crew," this is a term for any offender who works in a custodial job. "He is a unit swamper in A House." This term makes my girlfriend laugh.

switch IN/OUT:
to return to or leave your cell, as directed by a corrections officer.
"Even side, switch out for chow."

thirsty:
adjective used to describe someone who is desperate for something or acting selfish. "Some thirsty SOB bought all the popcorn out of the vending machine."

world:
any place outside of prison. "In the world, I was an accountant."

writ:
if you want the technical definition, find a dictionary. In prison speak, it is essentially a summons to appear in court and a reason to temporarily leave prison. People who "go on writ" generally have additional hearings and/or charges to attend to. "He went on a writ for a case he caught while on bail."

yard:
a general term for an outside area available to offenders for exercise, sports, etc. "We have yard at 9:50am on weekends."

yearlies:
the state allotment of prison clothes you are given annually. Generally, this includes socks, underwear, t-shirts, jeans, a long sleeved number and a coat and hat. Also, the cheapest pair of Rawlings white tennis shoes a person can buy at Pamida or Big Lots. That's right, the ones your great grandmother gave you for Easter when you were six.

ACKNOWLEDGEMENTS

At my sentencing, I made a promise to make the best of my incarceration for myself and others. I hope this handbook makes some progress toward that goal. From inside the prison walls, none of this would have been possible without the help, love and support of some amazing people. I cannot thank you enough.

To my kids Kate, Tony and Joe, and their mother Amy, thank you for standing by a broken man, loving him unconditionally and having such faith that he would make it out the other side in such a better, happier, place. I love you more than you could ever know. That first meal together is going to be the BEST.

To Em, I love you, sis. Thank you for everything you have done. Most importantly, thank you for believing in me. Warm up that smoker and get some crushed ice for the chalice.

To Kellie, no one understands us...whatever we are these days. But, we get each other and we understand, and that is all that matters. I will never, ever forget the love and strength you demonstrated through my crap, nor will I ever forget what your words felt like, and meant, at my prayer gathering. I hope you are proud of me. Lastly, thank you for bringing Chinese. @

To Scott, Mark and David......wow, how much you mean to me. You three amigos lifted a man from the depths of despair and brought him to Christ. I did not know any of you before my arrest and all you did was come along that monster on the news and show him unconditional love. I have learned so much from you and I am happy to pass it all on to others.

To my cellie Ty, we will be brothers for the rest of our lives. Only God could have brought us together. And, we will honor Him, together, as we share our testimony and minister to others. Get that cooler packed with sandwiches for our first road trip, buddy.

To the team who made this go from an idea, to a text, to an actual thing, many thanks. Shane, your artwork makes me smile and I so appreciate your time. That next time at Stadium View, I will keep your Coca-Cola and donuts refilled and deliver them to you in "the chair." Amy and Tony, this sounds ridiculous, but we have not met. Thank you for your time and assistance. When I waltz out these prison doors, I am picking you two up for breakfast at OPH and we will eat them out of bacon. Susan, thank you for all of your finishing touches. Don't ever stop calling me Dorway. I love that.

To Tina in the mailroom, thank you for doing your job so well. You saved this project. Literally.

To those who prayed, wrote, visited, took my calls, and followed my journey via Facebook, thank you for your grace and love for me and my family. Finishing my time would not have been possible without you. I hope you are proud of the man I have become and will continue to be.

Most importantly, I must give thanks to my savior Jesus Christ. I wish I had known you all along. But, you waited patiently for me, always at my side. It is because of you that I can confidently say I am no longer the disgraced former high school principal. I am a child of the living God.

ABOUT THE AUTHOR

Tim Dorway was sentenced to a 40 month sentence in the Minnesota Department of Corrections. His arrest on December 13, 2016 was the best day of his life.

While incarcerated, Tim completed a paralegal certification, took courses and programs offered in prison, and wrote and read extensively. He is blessed with a large support network and has worked to connect inmates in the system with mentors on the streets.

Tim plans to work in legal services as a paralegal. In addition, he would like to assist families and inmates with transitions to and from the prison system, as well as consult and support the families of currently incarcerated men and women. He also intends to share his testimony and help men struggling with sexual temptations, compulsions and addictions find support before it becomes too late.

In the future, Tim and his cellie Ty wish to bring together reformed sex offenders to do good in society, to find ways to support the victims of sex offenses and to effect change on society's impressions about the successes of reformed sex offenders upon release.

Made in the USA
Monee, IL
29 May 2023

34899985R00066